Influence

Student's Book

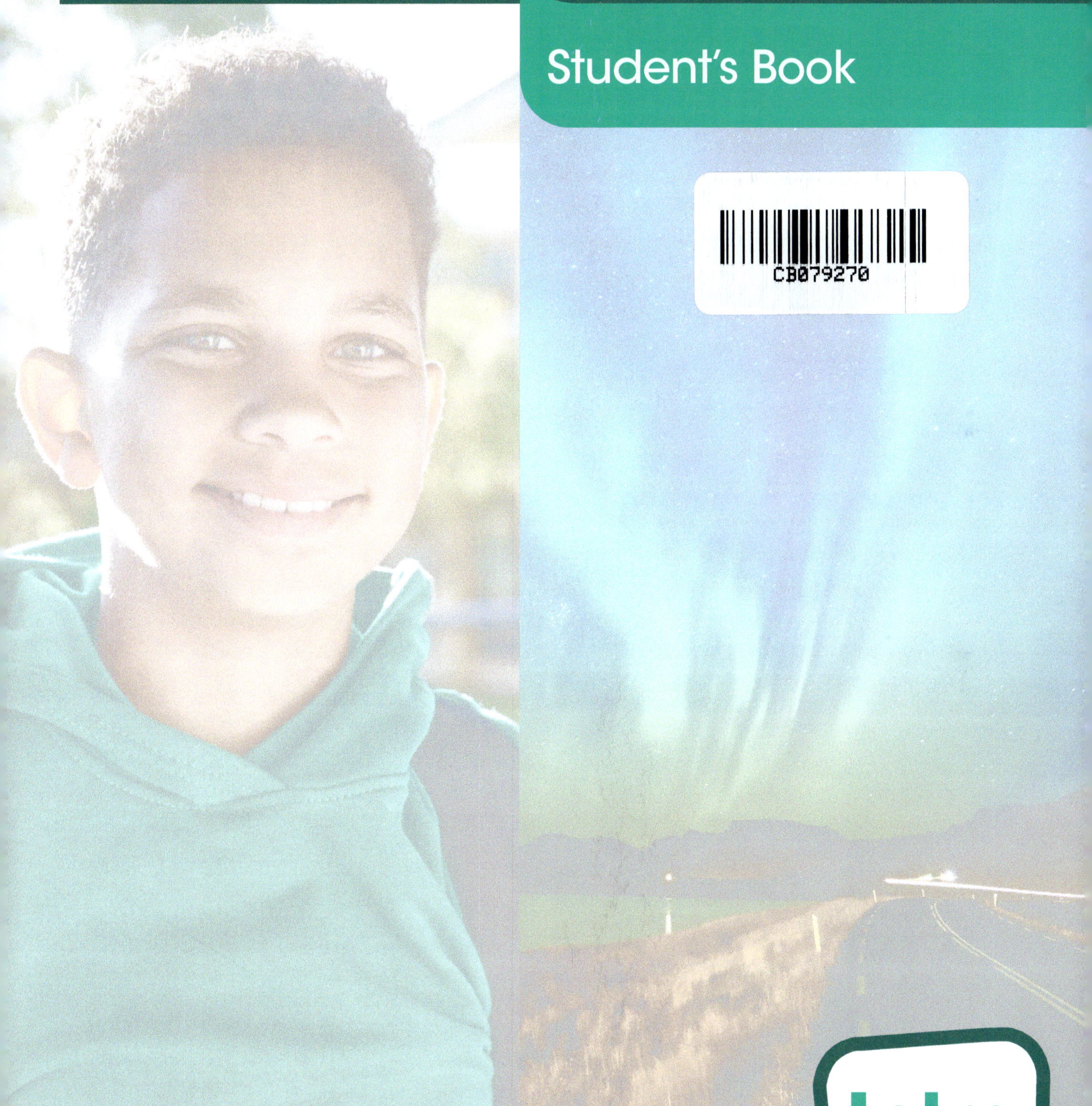

Intro

Gill Holley Kate Pickering

Influence

Projects

Collaborate with your classmates to develop your problem-solving skills in the WDYT? projects. Become an expert on a topic and influence others in your class.

WDYT?
(What do you think?)

Real-world content

Learn about culture while you learn English. *Influence* is full of real-world content so go online and learn more about the people, events and places in the book.

On-the-Go Practice

Access *Influence* On-the-Go Practice on your phone through the Macmillan Student's App to improve your English with gamified content. Collect points and improve your score each time you play.

Super skills

Influence helps develop your critical thinking, collaboration, creativity and communication skills which are essential for life in the 21st century.

COLLABORATION
CRITICAL THINKING
COMMUNICATION
CREATIVITY

SUPER SKILLS

Video

Influence videos help you with critical thinking, communication and project presentations and improve your video literacy skills.

Inclusive classroom

Learn at your own pace with reinforcement or challenge activities in the Grammar bootcamp. Show your strengths and talents by putting your investigative skills and logic to the test with *Influence* Brain teasers.

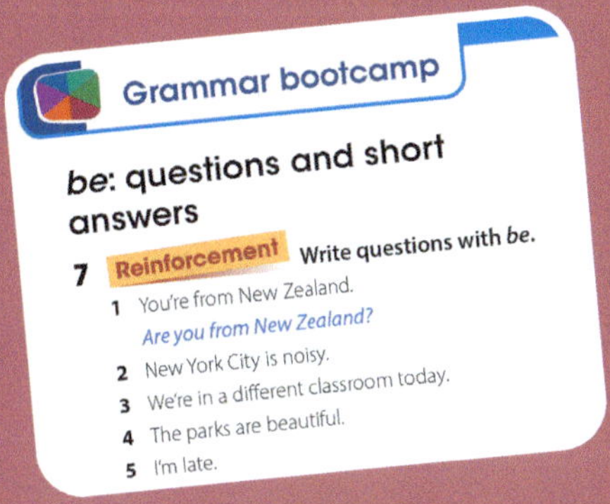
Grammar bootcamp

be: questions and short answers

7 Reinforcement Write questions with *be*.

1 You're from New Zealand.
Are you from New Zealand?
2 New York City is noisy.
3 We're in a different classroom today.
4 The parks are beautiful.
5 I'm late.

LISTENING	REAL-WORLD SPEAKING	WRITING	PRONUNCIATION	PROJECT
Grammar: subject pronouns and possessive adjectives, *a/an* and plurals, *this/that/these/those*, imperatives				
A phone conversation about New Zealand **Subskill:** Using visual clues	Meeting new people	**A keypal message** **Subskill:** Capital letters	Word stress	Design a new country and make a poster to introduce your country. **Creativity** *Using your imagination*
A radio programme about unusual twins **Subskill:** Using what you know	Talking about photos	**An email** **Subskill:** Apostrophes	/ə/	Make a circle map of important people in your life. **Critical thinking** *Thinking about things in different ways*
A street interview about shopping centres **Subskill:** Taking notes while you listen	Ordering food	**A blog post about food** **Subskill:** *and* and *but*	Silent letters	Plan your ideal meal. **Collaboration** *Working well together*
A conversation about a phone app **Subskill:** Listening to complete sentences	Making plans	**Notes and messages** **Subskill:** *because*	Pronouncing *-es* /ɪz/	Make a digital poster about a typical day. **Communication** *Asking for help and giving suggestions*
A talk about technology **Subskill:** Completing a table	Giving instructions	**An advert** **Subskill:** Spelling	Spelling the sound /iː/	Design a robot to solve a problem. **Creativity** *Finding new solutions to problems*
A radio programme from an art workshop **Subskill:** Using photo captions to help you understand	Asking for information	**Text messages** **Subskill:** *so*	/e/ and /ɜː/	Make a video guide for a photo exhibition. **Communication** *Communicating clearly*
A news report about teens and social media **Subskill:** Matching speakers with what they say	Talking about last weekend	**A description of a fictional character** **Subskill:** *also*	*was*: weak and strong form	Make a comic about an unknown hero. **Collaboration** *Researching information and deciding what to include*
A radio programme about Bike to School Week **Subskill:** Listening to choose the best summary	Buying a ticket	**A story** **Subskill:** *before* and *after*	Contracted forms	Do a class survey about transport and present the results. **Collaboration** *Deciding on roles in groupwork*
Listening: review of subskills		**Speaking:** review of Key phrases		**Writing:** review of subskills

Project planner p130 Irregular verbs p134

STARTER What do you know?

Back to school

Vocabulary: saying hello

1 **Look at the picture and complete the dialogue with the phrases in the box.**

I don't know	I'm fine	Hi Max

2 1 **Listen and check. Then practise the dialogue in pairs.**

3 **Match expressions 1–5 with expressions with a similar meaning a–e.**

1 Hello.
2 I'm fine.
3 I don't know.
4 Thank you.
5 Goodbye.

a Thanks.
b Bye.
c Hi.
d I'm not sure.
e I'm OK.

Grammar: subject pronouns and possessive adjectives

4 **The underlined words are subject pronouns. The words in bold are possessive adjectives. Copy and complete the table with words from the dialogue and in the box.**

Hi. I'm Callum. What's **your** name?

My name's Rob. We're in the same class.

he	her	it	their

Subject pronoun	Possessive adjective
I	**1** (…)
you	**2** (…)
3 (…)	his
she	**4** (…)
5 (…)	its
6 (…)	our
they	**7** (…)

5 **Choose the correct option.**

1 That's Mr King. He's **we/our** new English teacher.
2 Markus and Clare are new this year. **They/Their** are in our class.
3 **My/I** name's Mrs Clark and **my/I** 'm the headteacher.
4 **A:** Is this **you/your** chair?
B: No, I think **it's/its** free.
5 **A:** Where's Anisha?
B: **She/Her** isn't in **we/our** class this year.

Reinforcement and Challenge → Grammar bootcamp p116

What's in your bag?

Vocabulary: personal objects

1 Look at bags A–C. Match objects 1–7 with the words in the box.

bag books keys mobile phone money notebook pencil case

A

B

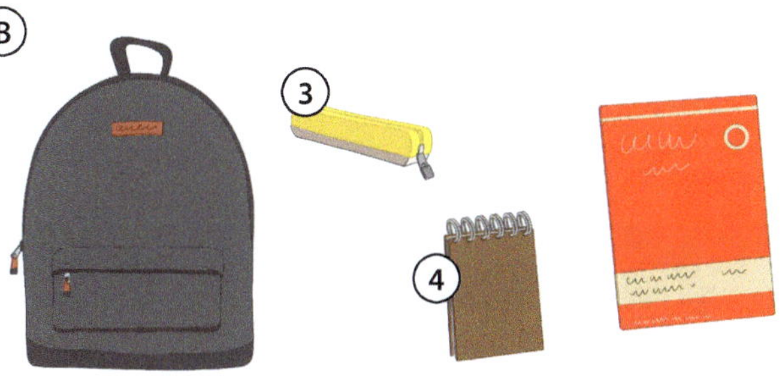

C

Grammar: *a*, *an* and plurals

2 Read the examples and the rules. Then write *a* or *an*.

***a* or *an*?**
Use *a* + singular noun starting with a consonant sound.
a teacher
Use *an* + singular noun starting with a vowel sound.
an apple

1 (…) mobile phone
2 (…) pencil case
3 (…) object
4 (…) bag
5 (…) elephant
6 (…) school
7 (…) email
8 (…) taxi

3 Copy and complete the table with two plural nouns from exercise 1.

Most nouns: add *-s*	animals **1** (…) **2** (…)
Nouns ending in *-ch*, *-sh*, *-s*, *-ss* or *-x*: add *-es*	buses
Nouns ending in consonant + *-y*: omit *-y* + add *-ies*	cities

4 Make the words in the box plural and add them to the table in exercise 3.

address bag bank boy class country monkey phone story

Vocabulary: colours

5 Match colours 1–11 with the words in the box.

black blue brown green grey orange pink purple red white yellow

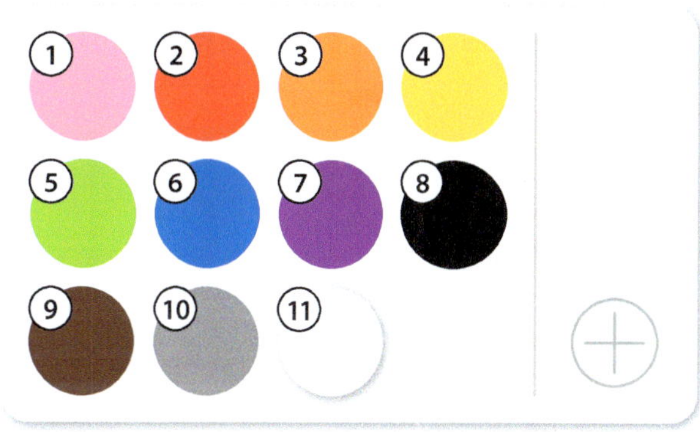

6 Work in pairs. Point to objects in the pictures in exercise 1 and ask about the colour.

What colour's the mobile phone in bag A?

It's orange.

7 2 Listen to three dialogues. Which bag is each dialogue about?

8 Work in pairs. What can your partner remember about his/her bag? Ask questions. Then look and check.

What's in your bag?

A mobile phone, my keys and a book.

What colour's the book?

I think it's black.

Reinforcement and Challenge → Grammar bootcamp p116

School days

Vocabulary: days of the week

1 Look at the calendar. Write the days of the week in the correct order. What day is the first day of school?

Friday Monday Saturday Sunday Thursday Tuesday Wednesday

SEPTEMBER

M	T	W	T	F	S	S
Back to school!		1	2	3	4	5
6	7	8	9	10	11	12
13	14	15	16	17	18	19
20	21	22	23	24	25	26
27	28	29	30			

2 🔊 3 Listen and repeat the days of the week.

3 Look at the calendar and write the day of the week for dates a–e.

a 4th **b** 8th **c** 2nd **d** 7th **e** 12th

Vocabulary: the classroom

4 Look at the two classrooms. Match objects 1–8 with the words in the box.

board chair ~~clock~~ computer desk door poster window

1 clock

ABOUT NEW POSTS ARCHIVES

WHAT'S YOUR IDEAL CLASSROOM?

POSTED 12TH AUGUST

5 Which classroom from exercise 4 do you prefer? Why?

6 Complete the description with words from exercise 4.

This is my ideal classroom. These are our tables. There are four **1** (...) at each table. This **2** (...) at the front of the class is for the teacher. That's the **3** (...) for the teacher to write on. We've got two **4** (...) . We use them to do projects. Those **5** (...) on the walls are our project work.

Grammar: *this, that, these, those*

7 **Read the sentences. Copy and complete the table with *This is*, *That's*, *These are* or *Those are*.**

This is my ideal classroom. These are our tables.
That's the board. Those are our computers.

Singular	1 *This is* a chair.	2 (…) a chair.
Plural	3 (…) chairs.	4 (…) chairs.

8 **Work in pairs. Student A, point at something in your classroom. Student B, say what it is using *this*, *that*, *these* or *those*.**

That's a clock.

These are our desks.

Instructions

Vocabulary: classroom instructions

1 **Match pictures 1–8 with instructions a–h.**

a Look at the board.
b Listen.
c Don't write the answer.
d Work in pairs.
e Open your books at page 11.
f Don't talk.
g Read the text.
h Copy this into your notebook.

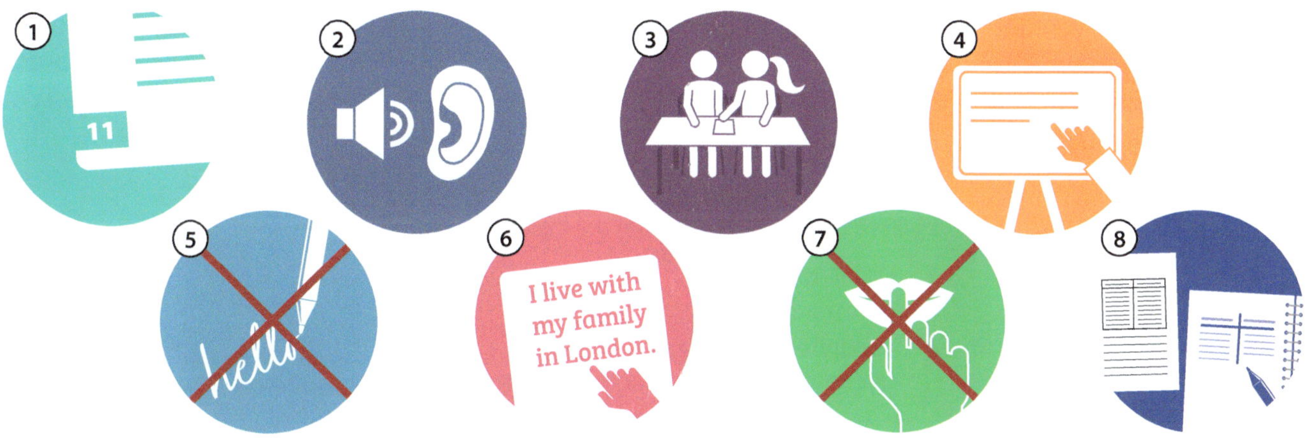

2 4 **Listen and follow the instructions.**

Grammar: imperatives

3 **Read the examples. Match 1–3 with a–c to make rules.**

Read the text. Don't talk.
Work in pairs. Don't write the answers.

1 We use imperatives
2 To make the imperative
3 To make the negative

a we use *don't* + infinitive.
b to give instructions.
c we use the infinitive.

4 **Complete the instructions with the affirmative (+) or negative (-) imperative form of the verbs in the box.**

~~copy~~ listen look open read work write

1 *Don't copy* the questions. **(-)**
2 (…) to the audio. **(+)**
3 (…) the answers in your book. **(-)**
4 (…) your books. **(-)**
5 (…) at the pictures on page 12. **(+)**
6 (…) the text. **(-)**
7 (…) in groups. **(+)**

5 **Work in pairs. Take turns to give instructions.**

Write the day today.

Don't look at the clock.

Open your book at page 50.

International English

Vocabulary: numbers 1–100

1 **Put the numbers in the box in order.**

eighteen eleven fifteen five seven six thirteen three twelve twenty two

2 **Write the missing numbers in exercise 1 from 1 to 20.**

3 **Write the numbers in the box as words.**

20 30 40 50 60 70 80 90 100

20 – twenty

4 5 **Listen and write the numbers as words.**

5 6 **Complete the information about English with the numbers from exercise 4. Then listen and check.**

Vocabulary: international words

6 **Add international words 1–8 to the correct category.**

- Animals
- Food
- Places
- Sports
- Technology

7 **Add the words in the box to the categories in exercise 6.**

chocolate computer football golf lion park phone rugby school

Vocabulary: the alphabet

8 7 **Listen and repeat the letters.**

A B C D E F G H I J
K L M N O P Q R S
T U V W X Y Z

9 **Work in pairs. Use the alphabet code (A = 1, B = 2, C = 3, ...) to decode the words.**

1 10.21.4.15 *10 = J, 21 = U, 4 = D, 15 = O – judo*
2 3.9.14.5.13.1
3 9.14.20.5.18.14.5.20
4 16.1.19.20.1
5 8.15.3.11.5.25
6 5.12.5.16.8.1.14.20

10 **Add the words in exercise 9 to the categories in exercise 6.**

1 judo – Sports

What's in this book?

1 **In which unit do you see photos 1–9?**

1 (...)

2 (...)

3 (...)

4 (...)

5 (...)

6 (...)

7 (...)

8 (...)

9 (...)

2 **Look through the Student's Book and find sections 1–6. Write the page number(s).**

1 a list of irregular verbs
2 pronunciation exercises
3 a project about a typical day
4 a grammar bootcamp
5 a review page about the past simple
6 graphic organisers for project support

3 **Work in pairs. Complete the challenge.**

Classroom CHALLENGE

How quickly can you find the answers?

1. What's the title of Unit 6?
2. What's the grammar on p66?
3. What's the project in Unit 3?
4. What's the writing task in Unit 8?
5. What's the title of the reading text in Unit 5?
6. What's the WDYT? question in Unit 7?
7. What's the pronunciation in Unit 1?
8. What's the vocabulary about on p77?
9. What's the speaking about in Unit 4?
10. What's the listening subskill in Unit 2?

1 Our world

WDYT? (What do you think?)

How are countries different?

Vocabulary: countries and nationality adjectives; adjectives to describe places

Grammar: *be* (affirmative, negative, questions and short answers)

Reading: informational texts about life in the Netherlands

Listening: a phone conversation about New Zealand

Speaking: meeting new people

Writing: a keypal message

Project: design a new country

Video skills p13

Real-world speaking p19

Project pp22–23

Countries and nationality adjectives

1 🔊 8 **Work in pairs. Complete the quiz and compare with your partner. Then listen and check.**

What about number 1?

I think it's the USA.

2 🔊 9 **Write the nationality for the countries in the quiz. Then listen, check and repeat.**

The USA, American

Language note

It's from Spain.

It's Spanish food.

Thank you ... for ...

These things are popular all around the world, but where do they come from?

1. **Thank you (...) for Hollywood.**
   a) the UK b) the USA c) Australia
2. **Thank you (...) for paper.**
   a) Mexico b) the UK c) China
3. **Thank you (...) for tapas.**
   a) Spain b) Australia c) Mexico
4. **Thank you (...) for Wi-Fi.**
   a) China b) the USA c) Australia
5. **Thank you (...) Sherlock Holmes.**
   a) the UK b) the USA c) Mexico
6. **Thank you (...) for chocolate.**
   a) China b) Mexico c) the UK

3 Work in pairs. Ask your partner about the things in exercise 1.

Where's paper from?

It's from China./It's Chinese.

4 Which continent is each country in? Which continent is missing?

5 Match the countries in the box to the continents in exercise 4.

Brazil India Japan the Netherlands
New Zealand Russia Turkey

6 Copy and complete the table with the nationality adjectives for the countries in exercise 5.

-an	*-ian*	*-ese*	*-ish*	Irregular
Mexican	Australian	Chinese	Spanish	6 *New Zealand*
American	1 (...)	4 (...)	British	7 *Dutch*
	2 (...)		5 (...)	
	3 (...)			

7 Complete the sentences with the correct country name or nationality adjective.

1 Sony is a brand from (...) .
2 Ajax is a (...) football team.
3 Cancún is a city in (...) .
4 Baseball is a popular (...) sport.
5 Moscow is the capital city of (...) .
6 Iberia is a (...) airline.

8 Work in pairs. Change the underlined words in exercise 7 to make new sentences with different countries and nationalities. Then test another pair.

VIDEO SKILLS

9 Watch the video. What are Isabel's top three places to visit?

10 Work in pairs. Answer the questions.

1 Why are travel videos interesting?
2 What is your favourite place in the video? Why?
3 What type of video are the lions in? Why?

Pronunciation: Word stress → p128

Informational texts

1 **Match words 1–5 with photos A–E.**

1 money
2 city transport
3 food
4 a popular sport
5 school

Subskill: Identifying different types of text

Before you read, look at the texts to help you understand what type of information they give you. Do you see: titles? pictures? complete sentences or words and numbers?

2 **Look at the four texts, but don't read them. Which text tells you …**

a general information about the Netherlands?
b unusual information about the Netherlands?
c about one Dutch teenager's life?
d about teenage life in general?

3 **Read the texts quickly. Which information in exercise 1 is not in the texts?**

4 10 **Read and listen to the texts. Match sentence halves 1–5 with a–e.**

1 Amsterdam is
2 Dutch people love
3 Thomas's parents are from
4 Most Dutch teens
5 Life at home and at school

a is good in the Netherlands.
b are happy.
c cycling.
d the capital of the Netherlands.
e different countries.

5 **Are the sentences true or false? Correct the false sentences.**

1 Thomas is 12 years old.
2 A typical Dutch person cycles 1,000 km a year.
3 Most Dutch teenagers are happy at school.
4 Thomas is from Zwolle.
5 Dutch food is bad for you.
6 75% of the Netherlands isn't under sea level.
7 It's difficult for teenagers to talk to their parents and teachers.

6 **Word work** **Match the definitions to the words in bold in the text.**

1 very good
2 everything connected with school and learning
3 the food people eat
4 an informal word for 'bicycle'
5 the things you study in school, e.g. English, maths
6 the money people use in a country, e.g. dollars

7 **Work in pairs. Ask and answer the questions about you and your country.**

1 What's the currency?
2 Name three things that are part of a good diet.
3 What's your favourite school subject?
4 Are bikes popular?
5 How old are children when they start education?
6 What's a great place to go with friends in your city?

CRITICAL THINKING

SUPER SKILLS

1 **Remember** Look at the texts. Find one thing which is similar to life in your country and one thing which is different.

2 **Evaluate** To be happy, what things do you think are important? Order the words:

education family free time food health money people the weather

THE NETHERLANDS:

a good place to be a teenager

1 **COUNTRY FACT FILE**

Name: The Netherlands

Population: 17 million

Nationality: Dutch

Capital city: Amsterdam

Currency: The euro

2 **MEET THOMAS**

Hi, I'm Thomas. I'm 13 years old. I'm half English and half Dutch. This is me and my brother – we're from Zwolle. I think the Netherlands is a **great** place to live.

3 **THE NUMBER ONE PLACE FOR HAPPY TEENAGERS IS ... THE NETHERLANDS.**

95% of Dutch teenagers say their life is good. Here are some of the reasons:

People:

People are open. It isn't difficult for Dutch teenagers to talk to their parents and teachers.

Food:

The Dutch **diet** is good for you.

Education:

Dutch schools are good. Most students are happy at school. It's easy to change **subjects** or repeat a year.

4 **QUICK FUN FACTS**

86% of Dutch people speak English as a second language.

25% of the country is under the sea! The top place in the Netherlands is just 323 m high.

The Dutch are **bike** crazy! A typical person cycles 900 km a year.

The longer read → Resource centre

be: affirmative

1 Read the examples. Copy and complete the table with the words in blue.

I'm 13 years old. We're from Zwolle.
The Dutch are bike crazy. 25% of the Netherlands is under the sea.

Full form			Contracted form	
I	am	from Turkey.	**3** (…)	12 years old.
You	**1** (…)		You're	
We			**4** (…)	
They			They're	
He	**2** (…)		He's	
She			She's	
It			It's	

2 Rewrite the dialogue with contracted forms.

Hi! I am Claudia and this is my friend, Jorge. He is 14. We are from Natal. It is a city in Brazil.

Hi Claudia. I am Berta and these are my friends, Lola and Julia. They are from Barcelona. I am from Valencia.

3 Rewrite the sentences with subject pronouns, contracted forms and nationality adjectives.

1 Daniel is from Mexico. *He's Mexican.*
2 Sara and María are from Spain.
3 Joe and I are from the USA.
4 Tatiana is from Russia.
5 I am from the UK.

4 11 **Choose the correct option. Listen and check. What's the answer to the final clue?**

Quiz: Where am I?

A: Ready? **1 I'm/I's** in a big city. **2 It're/It's** hot. I can see pyramids.
B: **3 You's/You're** in Cairo in Egypt.
A: OK, this time **4 we's/we're** in a city in Europe. I can see a big metal tower …
B: The Eiffel Tower! **5 We're/We'm** in Paris!
A: Fantastic. Now, I can see nine big letters: H-O-L-L-Y …
B: Hollywood – **6 it's/it are** in Los Angeles. **7 You'are/You're** in the USA!
A: Congratulations! This time I **8 're/'m** in a football stadium in a capital city in Europe. The players **9 is/are** in red and white. Atlético de …

be: negative

5 Read the examples. Copy and complete the table with the words in blue.

It isn't difficult to talk to parents and teachers.
Students aren't under a lot of pressure.

Subject	*be (+ not)*	
I	'm not (am not)	Dutch.
You/We/They	**1** (…) (are not)	
He/She/It	**2** (…) (is not)	

6 Change the sentences from affirmative to negative or negative to affirmative.

1 Cem is from Istanbul.
2 We aren't from Miami.
3 I'm Indian.
4 Elena isn't from Brazil.
5 You're from Tokyo.

7 Correct the sentences.

1 Washington is the capital of the Netherlands.
Washington isn't the capital of the Netherlands. It's the capital of the USA.
2 China and India are in Europe.
3 Thomas is from Spain.
4 We're in a maths class.
5 I'm British.

8 Complete the text with the correct contracted forms of *be*.

Today we **1** (…) **(+)** at the United Nations, but we **2** (…) **(-)** in New York. We're in Madrid and the people here **3** (…) **(-)** adults, they're teenagers. Welcome to the SEK Model United Nations. It **4** (…) **(+)** an event for students in high school. I **5** (…) **(+)** with some students from the USA. It's their first time in Madrid, but they **6** (…) **(-)** here to visit the Santiago Bernabéu Stadium. They **7** (…) **(+)** here to discuss important questions and understand other countries better.

9 Answer the question to solve the Brain teaser.

BRAIN TEASER

The first letter of each answer spells a country.

1 People from the UK are *British*: *B*
2 St Petersburg is in this country.
3 The capital of Turkey is (…) .
4 Zambia and (…)imbabwe are in Africa.
5 New Delhi is the capital of this country.
6 The capital of the UK is (…) .

What is the country?

Reinforcement and Challenge → Grammar bootcamp p117

Adjectives to describe places

1 Look at the tourist information. Is New Zealand a good place to visit? Why?

2 Match the words in yellow in exercise 1 with their opposites in the box.

cold dangerous dirty empty interesting noisy old ~~ugly~~

beautiful – ugly

Adjectives

Adjectives come before a noun or after the verb *be*. They are never plural.

Auckland is	*a modern city* ✓	~~*a city modern*~~ ✗
The beaches aren't	*crowded* ✓	~~*crowdeds*~~ ✗

3 Work in pairs. Complete the sentences about your town/city.

1 My town/city is (…) and (…) .
2 It's a/an (…) place to visit.
3 The centre is (…) and (…) .
4 In summer it's (…) and in winter it's (…) .
5 My favourite place in the town/city is (…) because it's (…) and (…) .

A phone conversation

Subskill: Using visual clues

Titles, photos and maps all give information about a listening. Look at these before you listen.

4 Look at the photos. What do they tell you about New Zealand?

5 12 Listen to a conversation and choose the correct option.

1 New Zealand **is/isn't** a small country.
2 Auckland **is/isn't** the capital city.
3 Maori **is/isn't** the only language.

6 Listen again. Are the sentences true or false?

1 New Zealand and the UK are about the same size.
2 Most people live on the South Island.
3 Wellington is a big city.
4 New Zild is English with Maori words.
5 For Chloe, New Zealand is a boring place.
6 Sports are popular in New Zealand.

7 Complete the notes.

Population	**1** (…) million
Capital city	**2** (…)
Weather	**3** (…) in summer **4** (…) in winter on the South Island
Official languages	**5** (…) and Maori
National sport	**6** (…)

8 Work in pairs. Is New Zealand similar to or different from your country? Why?

It's different because it's a small country, and we live in a big country.

fun facts A person from New Zealand is a 'Kiwi.' A kiwi is a type of bird from the country (not the fruit!).

Vocabulary extension → Workbook p100

be: questions and short answers

1 **Read the questions and short answers. Copy and complete the table.**

Is New Zealand a big country? No, it isn't.
Are the winters cold? No, they aren't.
Are you happy there? Yes, I am.

Question	Short answers
Am I from New Zealand?	Yes, I **1** (…) . / No, I'm not.
2 (…) you happy there?	Yes, you are. / No, you aren't.
Is New Zealand a big country?	Yes, it is. / No, it **3** (…) .
Are we Kiwis?	Yes, we are. / No, we aren't.
4 (…) the winters cold?	Yes, they are. / No, they **5** (…) .

Short answers: contracted forms

We don't use contracted forms in affirmative short answers.

Yes, I am. ✓ ~~*Yes, I'm.*~~ ✗
Yes, it is. ✓ ~~*Yes, it's.*~~ ✗

But we use contracted forms in negative short answers.

No, I'm not. *No, it isn't.*

2 **Order the words to make questions.**

1 is / big / your city ?
2 happy / are / you and your classmates ?
3 from the USA / is / your teacher ?
4 you / are / from / Japan ?
5 summers in your country / hot / are ?

3 **Match the questions in exercise 2 with answers a–e.**

a Yes, she is.
b No, they aren't.
c Yes, I am.
d No, it isn't.
e Yes, we are.

4 13 **Complete the dialogue, then listen and check.**

Lily: **1** (…) you from New Zealand?
Erin: No, I **2** (…) . I'm from the USA.
Lily: **3** (…) your parents from the USA?
Erin: No, they **4** (…) . They're from Shanghai in China.
Lily: **5** (…) Shanghai a small city?
Erin: No, it **6** (…) . It's very big! The population is about 26 million.
Lily: **7** (…) you and your family happy in the USA?
Erin: Yes, we **8** (…) . Very happy!

5 14 **Listen to the questions and write true answers for you.**

6 **Choose the correct option.**

GRAMMAR ROUND-UP

1 2 3 4 5 6 7 8

MESSAGEBOARD Log in

All flags **1 is/are** different, but most flags are red, blue or white.

Is the colour of a flag important?
2 12 41

Yes, **2 they are/it is**. The Japanese flag is white with a red circle. The circle is a symbol of the Sun.
2 6 24

3 You are/Are you from Japan?
4 20 18

No, I **4 isn't/'m not**. I'm from New Zealand.
4 20 18

Is the New Zealand flag the same as the Australian flag?
0 8 16

No, it **5 is/isn't**. The New Zealand flag has got four stars, and the Australian flag has got six stars.
2 5 36

Are all flags rectangles?
8 2 74

No, they **6 isn't/aren't**. For example, the flag from Nepal **7 is/are** the only one with five sides.
1 63 92

Research

Choose a country and find the flag. Describe it to your classmates.

Reinforcement and Challenge → Grammar bootcamp p118

Meeting new people

1 Watch the video. Are the girls friends?

2 Watch again. Which Key phrases do you hear?

3 Complete the dialogue with the Key phrases. Watch again and check.

Elena: Hi there! Are you new here?

Amy: Hi. Yes, I am. This is my first day.

Elena: Welcome to Bedford High! **1** (…) name?

Amy: **2** (…) Amy.

Elena: I'm Elena. Where **3** (…), Amy? Are you Australian?

Amy: No, **4** (…) Portland, in the USA.

Elena: Is that a big city?

Amy: No, it isn't. It's small and quiet. **5** (…) you, Elena?

Elena: **6** (…) 12.

Amy: Me too.

Elena: Oh, here's Mr West. He's our French teacher. See you later!

Amy: OK. See you!

4 Create your own dialogue. Follow the steps in the Skills boost.

SKILLS BOOST

THINK

Work individually. Invent a new identity and make notes.

- Name
- Age
- Country/Nationality
- City

PREPARE

In pairs, prepare a dialogue. You meet a new student in your school. Use the information from your new identities. Remember to use Key phrases for meeting new people.

Hi there! Are you new here?

Yes, I am.

PRACTISE

Practise your dialogue.

PERFORM

Act out your dialogue for the class.

5 **Peer review** Listen to your classmates and answer the questions.

1 Are the Key phrases correct?

2 Where are the new students from?

Key phrases

What's your name?	My name's … / I'm …
Good/Nice to meet you.	You too!
Where are you from?	I'm from …
How old are you?	I'm (12/13).

Real-world grammar

Are you new here? Yes, I am.

I'm from Portland, in the USA.

Is that a big city? No, it isn't. It's small and quiet.

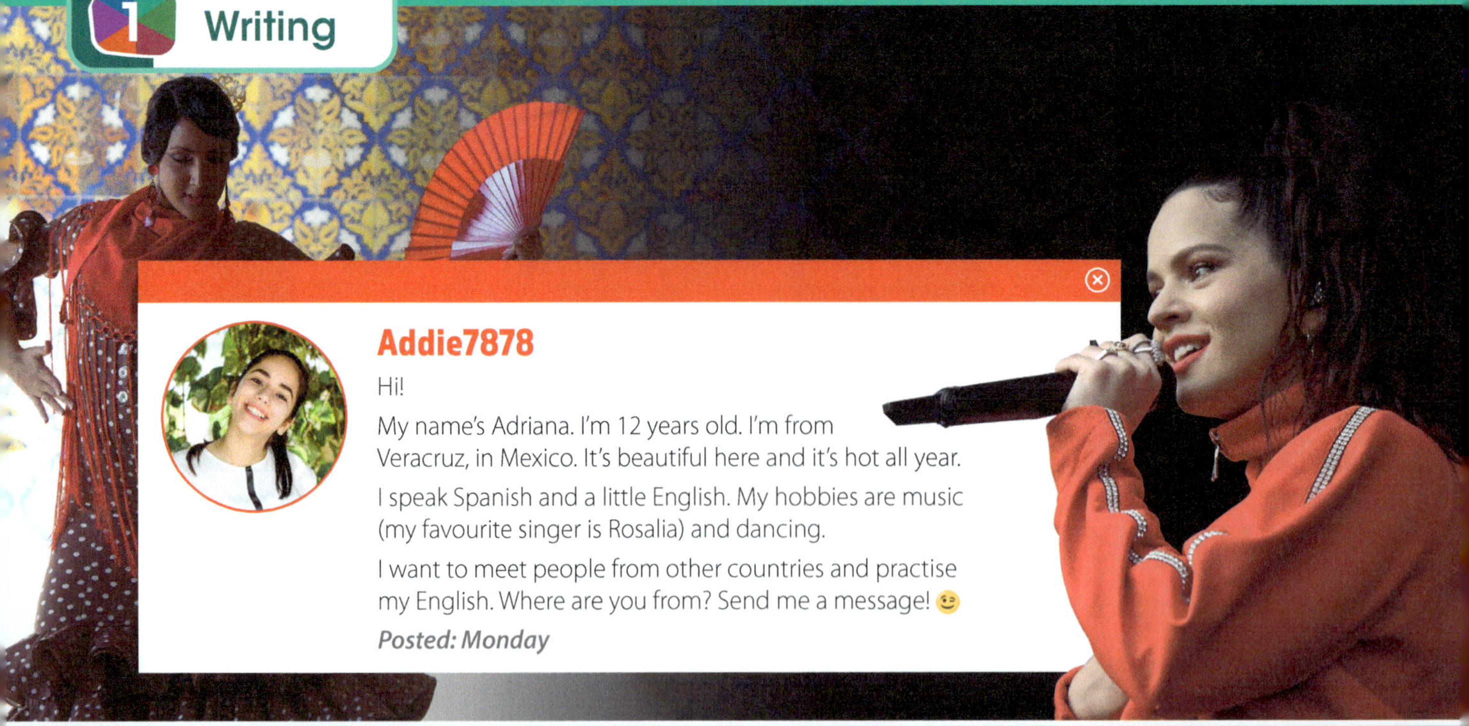

Addie7878

Hi!

My name's Adriana. I'm 12 years old. I'm from Veracruz, in Mexico. It's beautiful here and it's hot all year.

I speak Spanish and a little English. My hobbies are music (my favourite singer is Rosalia) and dancing.

I want to meet people from other countries and practise my English. Where are you from? Send me a message! 😉

Posted: Monday

Ken_TYO

Hi there!

My name's Kenji. I'm Japanese. I'm from Tokyo, the capital city of Japan. It's a big, BIG city on the island of Honshu.

I'm 11 years old. My hobbies are sports and manga. My favourite sports are judo and baseball. I speak Japanese and English.

I want to make friends in other countries. Write to me!

Posted: Friday

A keypal message

1 **Read the two keypal messages. Choose the message you prefer. Why?**

2 **Read the messages again. Copy and complete the profiles.**

Profile application

A	B
Name:	**Name:**
Age:	**Age:**
Country:	**Country:**
Nationality:	**Nationality:**
City:	**City:**
Languages:	**Languages:**
Hobbies:	**Hobbies:**

▶ Subskill: Capital letters

In English, some words have a capital letter. These include the first letter of a sentence, the pronoun *I*, countries and nationalities, and days of the week.

3 **Find two examples for each rule in the messages. We use capital letters for …**

1 the pronoun *I*
2 countries and nationalities
3 cities
4 languages
5 days of the week
6 the first word in a sentence or question
7 names

Writing competence → Workbook pp108–109

4 **Rewrite the sentences with capital letters where necessary.**

1 i'm from india.
2 i speak portuguese and french.
3 istanbul is a big, beautiful city in turkey.
4 i'm half dutch and half german.
5 my favourite day of the week is saturday.
6 i live in moscow, the capital city of russia.

5 **Find expressions in the messages to …**

1 start a message
2 say why you want a keypal
3 ask people to write to you

6 **Write a message to ask for a keypal. Follow the steps in the Skills boost.**

SKILLS BOOST

THINK

Look at the profile information in exercise 2. Make notes about you.

PREPARE

Make notes to describe your city.

Make notes about your favourite singer, sport, day of the week, etc.

WRITE

Write your keypal message. Remember to include an expression to:

- start your message
- say why you want a keypal
- ask people to write to you

CHECK

Check your work. Pay attention to:

- the present simple of *be*
- capital letters

7 **Peer review** **Exchange your keypal message with other students. Answer the questions.**

1 Is *be* correct?
2 Are the capital letters correct?
3 Choose one person to be your keypal. Say why.

Grammar

be

Affirmative

I am	I'm
He/She/It is	He/She/It's
We/You/They are	We/You/They're

I'm (am) from Turkey.
He's (is) 12 years old.

Negative

I am not	I'm not
He/She/It is not	He/She/It isn't
We/You/They are not	We/You/They aren't

*I'm **not** from Spain.*
*He **isn't** 14 years old.*

Questions and short answers

Am I … ?	Yes, I am. / No, I'm not.
Is he/she/it … ?	Yes, he/she/it is. No, he/she/it isn't.
Are we/you/they … ?	Yes, we are. / No, we aren't.
***Are you** from Japan?*	*No, **I'm not**.*
***Is he** Dutch?*	*Yes, he **is**.*

Contracted forms

We don't use contracted forms in affirmative short answers, but we use contracted forms in negative short answers.

Yes, I am.	*Yes, it is.*
No, I'm not.	*No, it isn't.*

Vocabulary

15 Countries and nationality adjectives

Australia – Australian
China – Chinese
Japan – Japanese
New Zealand – New Zealand
Spain – Spanish
the UK – British
Turkey – Turkish
Brazil – Brazilian
India – Indian
Mexico – Mexican
Russia – Russian
the Netherlands – Dutch
the USA – American

16 Adjectives to describe places

beautiful/ugly, clean/dirty, empty/crowded, hot/cold, interesting/boring, modern/old, quiet/noisy, safe/dangerous

1 Project

WDYT?
(What do you think?)

How are countries different?

TASK: Design a new country and make a poster to introduce your country.

Learning outcomes

1 I can design and present a poster about a country.

2 I can use creativity and my imagination.

3 I can use appropriate language from the unit.

Graphic organiser → Project planner p130

1 Watch a video of students presenting their poster. Where is Calobia?

STEP 1: THINK

2 Look at the poster about a country in the Model project. What information does it include?

- language
- currency
- information about the flag
- a description
- important cities
- family life
- famous people
- food
- sports and hobbies
- school life
- population
- where the country is
- popular music
- unusual information

3 Now think about how the poster looks. Which things are in the poster?

- a title
- section headings
- drawings
- photos
- graphs and tables
- a map
- different fonts or styles of letters
- one big text
- several small texts

STEP 2: PLAN

4 Work in groups of three. Read the tips in the Super skills box and practise saying the Key phrases with your group.

CREATIVITY SUPER SKILLS

Using your imagination

Tips

Be original.

Think about your real country (name, currency, national sport, etc.). Then think about how to change them for your new country.

Don't choose the first idea. Think about other options too.

Key phrases

What's a good name/flag/national sport?

I like that/your/Sara's idea.

What about (Calobia)?

That's a good idea!

That's great!

No, that's not very original.

5 In your groups, choose five sections for your poster. Use the ideas in the Model project, or your own. Use the tips and Key phrases in the Super skills box.

6 Discuss each section and write some notes.

FLAG red – white – green (red = sun, ...)

7 Choose a person to prepare each section.

Student 1 – the flag, Fun Facts ...

Student 2 – map, important cities ...

Student 3 – language, currency ...

Grammar and Vocabulary → Quick review p21

Model project

COUNTRY FACT FILE

Nationality: Calobian
Languages: English and Calob
Capital city: Beachtown
Population: 25,000
Currency: Calobian dollar
Continent: Oceania

DESCRIPTION

Calobia is a small island in the Pacific Ocean. It's about 3,000 km from New Zealand. It's very beautiful and it's hot all year. The capital is Beachtown. It's a quiet place, but it isn't boring. Life in Calobia is very good.

Calobia

WHAT'S POPULAR IN CALOBIA?

National sport: Surfing
Popular food: Fish and pineapples
Famous people:
Luke Wobda (actor)
Maggie Filfo (surfer, rapper)

FUN FACTS

The president of Calobia is only 19 years old.

In Calobia you go to school on Saturday and Sunday and the weekend is Monday to Friday.

The octopus is a popular pet!

FLAG

The Calobian flag is dark blue, light blue and yellow.

Dark blue is for the sea, light blue is for the sky. Yellow is for the sun.

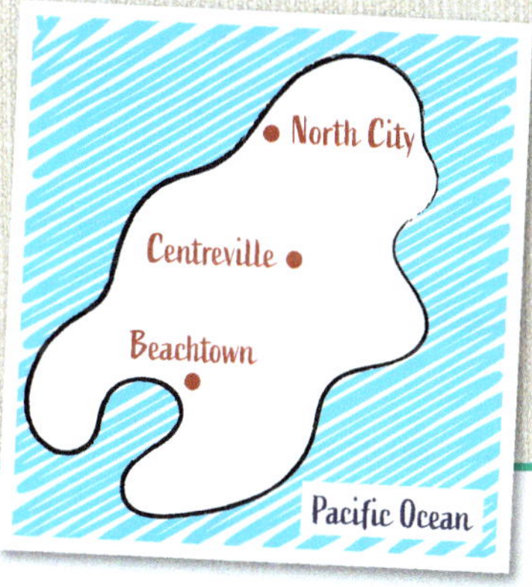

STEP 3: CREATE

8 Prepare the texts and visuals for your poster.

9 Read the *How to …* tips on p130. Then work together to organise your materials and create your poster.

STEP 4: PRESENT

10 **Peer review** Show and explain your poster to another group. As you listen, answer the questions.

1 How is the new country different from your real country?
2 Do you want to visit this country? Why/Why not?

1 FINAL REFLECTION

1 The task
Do you have a clear and attractive poster with information about your country?

2 Super skill
Do you use your imagination to find original ideas? Give examples.

3 Language
Do you use language from the unit? Give examples.

2 Family

The SEVEN FAMILIES game is from France. It's over 100 years old! Players try to collect all the cards of a family. It's a great game to play with family and friends!

WDYT? (What do you think?)

What is a family?

Vocabulary: family; describing people; parts of the body and face; describing hair

Grammar: *have got*: affirmative and negative; possessive *'s* and *s'*; *have got*: questions and short answers

Reading: a TV guide about a family in a reality show

Listening: a radio programme about unusual twins

Speaking: talking about photos

Writing: an email

Project: make a circle map of important people in your life

THE SEVEN FAMILIES GAME

Video skills p25

Real-world speaking p31

Project pp34–35

Family; describing people

1 **Read about the Seven Families game and answer the questions.**

1 Where is the game from?
2 How old is it?
3 Is the game popular in your country? What is it called?

2 **Look at the family tree. Complete the sentences with the words in the box.**

brother daughter father ~~mother~~ sister son

1 Louise is Paul's *mother*.
2 Lena is Martin's (...) .
3 Martin is Paul's (...) .
4 Anna is Louise's (...) .
5 Martin is Lena's (...) .
6 Victor is Paul's (...) .

Language note

father and mother = parents

son and daughter = children

A person with no brothers or sisters is **an only child**.

3 Write the name of the speaker.

1 'Paul and Anna are my **children**. Anna is my daughter and Paul is my son. Hugo is my **grandson**.'

2 'Louise is my **grandmother**. My **parents** are Sandra and Paul. Pierre is my **uncle**, Martin is my **brother** and Hugo is my **cousin**.'

3 'Paul is my brother. Martin is my **nephew** and Lena is my **niece**.'

4 Match male family members 1–8 with female equivalents a–h.

1 father	**a** daughter
2 brother	**b** cousin
3 grandfather	**c** aunt
4 son	**d** niece
5 uncle	**e** mother
6 grandson	**f** grandmother
7 nephew	**g** sister
8 cousin	**h** granddaughter

5 Complete the sentences with family words.

1 My sister's daughter is my *niece*.

2 My father's sister is my (...) .

3 My mother's father is my (...) .

4 My father's brother is my (...) .

5 My aunt's son is my (...) .

6 My sister's daughter is my (...) .

6 Match the adjectives in the box with photos A–C.

dark fair old short tall young

7 Match a person in your family (or a family in a TV series or film) with each of the adjectives in exercise 6. Compare your answers in pairs.

old: my grandfather (he's 79)

VIDEO SKILLS

8 Watch the video and answer the questions.

1 Who is the narrator? How old is he?

2 What is this video for, and why is it a good way to do this?

3 What is the answer to the last question in the video?

Pronunciation: /ə/ → p128

A TV guide

1 **Work in pairs. Look at the photos on p27. Answer the questions.**

1 Do you think the Putmans are a big family or a small family?
2 Why do you think this family is unusual?

Subskill: Predicting what a text is about

Look at the photos and text type. Think about what is in the text before you read it. This can help you understand a text when you read.

2 17 **Read and listen to the TV guide article. Check your answers in exercise 1.**

3 **Read the article again and complete the sentences.**

1 The Putmans are from (…) .
2 They all live in one (…) .
3 Bill and Barb are the (…) of the family.
4 They've got (…) children and (…) grandchildren.
5 The Putmans' house is (…) .
6 The children go to school in the family (…) .
7 The Putmans eat together at (…) o'clock every evening.

4 **Are the sentences true or false? Correct the false sentences.**

1 Bill and Barb have got two daughters.
2 The Putmans use two bathrooms.
3 Each child has got a separate bedroom.
4 The children study together in the evenings.
5 The Putmans eat at one big table.
6 The home is very quiet.

5 **Word work** **Match the definitions to the words in bold in the text.**

1 sad because you aren't with other people
2 with other people
3 not normal or typical
4 use or have with another person
5 a TV programme about the lives of real people
6 an adjective to describe an activity that you like

6 **Use the words in exercise 5. Write …**

1 the name of a reality show in your country
2 an activity that is fun
3 a place you and your friends go together
4 an unusual name for a boy or girl
5 an object that you share with a friend
6 something you do when you're lonely

7 **Work in pairs. Compare your answers in exercise 6. Are any answers the same?**

Big Brother is a reality show.

You're right! So is the music show *The Voice*.

8 **Read what the people say about their families. Answer the questions.**

I haven't got any brothers or sisters. I've got friends, but I'd love a sister to talk to. ***Eli, 11***

I've got two brothers, and they're very annoying! ***Clara, 13***

I'm an only child, but my dad has got six brothers and sisters. It's great because I've got a lot of cousins to do things with. ***Toby, 12***

1 Who … ?
 a is an only child
 b is happy with his/her situation (Why?)
 c isn't happy with his/her situation (Why?)
2 Who's got a situation similar to you? Why?

CRITICAL THINKING SUPER SKILLS

1 **Understand** Read the text again. Find two advantages and two disadvantages of a big family.

Advantages

The children help each other with their homework.

Disadvantages

The children share a bedroom.

2 **Apply** Think of two advantages and two disadvantages of a small family.

3 **Evaluate** What do you think is the ideal number of people in a family? Why?

Research

Find other TV programmes about families.

TV Guide

Meet the Putmans

+ add to watchlist

The Putmans are a big, happy family. That's not **unusual**, but all 26 people in this family live in one house! Every day is interesting in the Putman family, and you can see them in this **reality show**.

The grandparents' names are Bill and Barb Putman. They've got three sons and a daughter: Billy, Brandon, Blake and Blair (yes, all the names begin with the letter 'B'!). The four children are married, with children of their own. In total, Bill and Barb have got 16 grandchildren!

The Putmans live in Montana in the USA. It's a big family, but their house is small. It's only got two bathrooms, and the children haven't got their own bedroom. They **share** a room with their brothers and sisters.

And the Putmans haven't got a car – they've got a bus! The parents use it to take the children to school.

But the children are never **lonely**. They've got a lot of brothers, sisters and cousins to play with. They help each other with their homework after school. Then at six o'clock every evening, they eat **together** with their parents at three big tables.

The Putman home is noisy, but it's **fun**. Watch them tonight at eight o'clock.

fun facts Pavel Semenyuk from Ukraine has got 13 children, 127 grandchildren, 203 great-grandchildren and three great-great grandchildren. That's a Guinness World Record!

The longer read → Resource centre

have got: affirmative and negative

1 Read the examples. Copy and complete the table with the words in blue.

I've got a lot of cousins.
I haven't got any brothers or sisters.
It's got two bathrooms.
They've got three sons and a daughter.
The Putmans haven't got a car.

	Affirmative	Negative	
I	**1** (…)	**2** (…)	
You	've got	haven't got	a brother.
He/She/It	**3** (…)	hasn't got	a lot of
We	've got	haven't got	cousins.
They	**4** (…)	**5** (…)	

2 Match contracted forms 1–4 with long forms a–d.

1 've got
2 hasn't got
3 haven't got
4 's got

a have not got
b has got
c have got
d has not got

3 Complete the sentences with the affirmative or negative form of *have got*. Use contracted forms where possible.

1 My mum (…) two sisters. **(+)**
2 We (…) a big house. **(-)**
3 I (…) four cousins. **(+)**
4 My brother (…) a friend in the USA. **(+)**
5 My cousin (…) her own room. **(-)**
6 My aunt and uncle (…) a new car. **(+)**

Possessive *'s and s'*

4 Read the examples. Match sentence halves 1–3 with a–c to make rules.

The grandparents' names are Bill and Barb.
Their daughter's name is Blair.
Their sons' names are Billy, Brandon and Blake.
Toby's father has got six brothers and sisters.

1 We use *'s* and *s'*
2 After singular nouns,
3 After plural nouns ending in *-s*,

a we add *'*.
b to talk about possession and family.
c we add *'s*.

5 Write the underlined word with a possessive *'s* or *s'*.

1 My uncle Tom is my mums brother.
2 My grandparents house is very small.
3 My dads car is 15 years old.
4 My cousins names are Sam and Eva.
5 My parents birthdays are both in June.
6 My friend Lucys cat is called Missy.

6 Choose the correct option.

NEWS | ENTERTAINMENT | ARTICLES

Family is very important to the actor Will Smith. He's married to Jada Pinkett and he **1 've/'s** got two sons and a daughter. They all live in Los Angeles, and they **2 've/'s** all got jobs in music or films.

His **3 son's/sons'** names are Trey and Jaden. Jaden is a rapper and an actor, and he **4 've/'s** got his own clothes brand. Trey is a music producer. The brothers **5 haven't/hasn't** got any children. His **6 daughter's/daughters'** name is Willow and she's an actor and a singer. **7 Will's/Wills'** wife is also an actor.

Will **8 haven't/hasn't** got a big family, but they're all very famous!

7 Answer the question to solve the Brain teaser.

BRAIN TEASER

Eva and Megan (two girls) and Paolo and Greg (two boys) are all friends.

	has got a brother	has got a sister
Eva		
Megan		
Paolo		
Greg		

One boy has got a brother and a sister.
The girl with a brother hasn't got a sister.
Paolo is an only child.
Eva has got a sister, but she hasn't got a brother.

Can you describe the girls' and boys' families?

Reinforcement and Challenge → Grammar bootcamp p118

Parts of the body and face; describing hair

1 **Match the words in the box with parts of the body 1–5. Which word has an irregular plural?**

arm foot hand head leg

2 **Look at the app and match pictures 1–10 with the words in the box.**

beard ear eye hair moustache mouth nose short straight teeth

3 **Look at the avatar in exercise 1 and choose the correct description.**

1 Alice has got a big nose and blue eyes. She's got long, brown hair.
2 Alice has got blue eyes. She's got a small mouth and long, curly hair.
3 Alice has got long, straight hair and big brown eyes.

A radio programme

4 **Write a short description of the two girls in the photo. Then compare your description with your partner's.**

Subskill: Using what you know

Think about what you know about the subject before you listen. This will help you to understand.

5 **What do you know about twins? Are the sentences true or false?**

1 Twins are two children born at the same time.
2 There are two types of twins: identical and non-identical.
3 Twins are always the same sex: two boys or two girls.
4 Twins always look the same.

6 18 **Listen to a radio programme and check your answers in exercise 5.**

7 **Listen again. Who are the people? Complete the sentences with the words in the box. There is one extra word.**

a doctor a father a mother a twin (x2)

1 Sally is (...) .
2 Mr Aylmer is (...) .
3 Maria is (...) .
4 Lucy is (...) .

8 **Write the hair and eye colour of each person in the family.**

1 Lucy
2 Maria
3 Their father
4 Their mother

9 **Work in pairs. Ask and answer the questions.**

1 Do you know any twins?
2 Are they the same or different? (body, face, personality)
3 Say one advantage and one disadvantage of being a twin.

Vocabulary extension → Workbook p101

have got: questions and short answers

1 Copy and complete the table with the examples in the box.

Has she got blue eyes? No, she hasn't.
Have you got any interesting examples? Yes, I have.

Have	I/you/we/they	got … ?
Have	you	got a brother?
1 (…)	2 (…)	3 (…) ?
Yes,/No,	**I/you/we/they**	**have./haven't.**
4 (…) ,	5 (…)	6 (…) .
No,	I	haven't.

Has	he/she/it	got … ?
Has	he	got curly hair?
7 (…)	8 (…)	9 (…) ?
Yes,/No,	**he/she/it**	**has./hasn't.**
Yes,	he	has.
10 (…) ,	11 (…)	12 (…) .

2 Choose the correct option.

1 a Do you got a sister? b Have you got a sister?
2 a Yes, I have. b Yes, I've.
3 a Has your father got a beard? b Have your father got a beard?
4 a No, he have not. b No, he hasn't.

3 Look at the information and write all possible questions and answers with *have got*.

Has	sisters	a beard	long hair
you	Yes	No	Yes
your aunt	No	No	Yes
your cousins	No	Yes	No

Have you got any sisters? *Yes, I have.*

Language note

Have you got + *a*/*an* + singular noun
Have you got a beard?

Have you got + *any* + plural noun
Have you got any cousins?

4 Write questions with *have got* and *a*/*an* or *any*.

1 you / brothers or sisters ?
2 you / lucky number ?
3 you / favourite team ?
4 you / pets ?
5 you / favourite colour ?

5 Work in pairs. Ask and answer the questions in exercise 4.

6 19 Complete the dialogue with the correct form of *have got*. Then listen and check.

Charlie: Liam, **1** (…) a pen? **(you)**
Liam: Yes, **2** (…) . Here you are. **(I)**
Charlie: **3** (…) any pencils? **(you)**
Liam: No, **4** (…) . **(I)**
Charlie: **5** (…) any pencils? **(Jodie)**
Liam: I don't know. Jodie, **6** (…) any pencils? **(you)**
Jodie: Yes, **7** (…) . What colour? **(I)**
Charlie: **8** (…) a blue pencil? **(you)**
Jodie: Sure. Here you are.

7 Choose the correct option.

GRAMMAR ROUND-UP

1 2 3 4 5 6 7 8

Ask Alex Home | Answer | Search

Today's subject is TWINS

QUESTION: Are twins' birthdays always on the same day? **(Luke, Poland)**

ALEX: No, they **1 aren't/are**. Sometimes one baby is born before midnight and the other baby after midnight. **2 They/Their** birthdays are on two different days.

Q: **3 Is it/It is** possible for twins to have birthdays in different years? **(Chloe, Spain)**

A: **4 Yes, it's./Yes, it is.** The Shay twins from Arizona are non-identical: Sawyer **5 got/has got** dark brown hair. His brother Everett is fair. But that's not the only difference. The twins **6 has got/have got** birthdays in different years. **7 Sawyer's/Sawyer** birthday is on 31st December and Everett's is on 1st January.

Q: **8 Have you got/You have** any more crazy twin stories? **(Shanisa, Mexico)**

A: **9 Yes, I've got./Yes, I have.** Indianapolis twins Jacob and Jordan Wallman have got birthdays in different centuries! Jacob's date of birth is 31.12.1999 and his sister Jordan's is 01.01.2000!

Reinforcement and Challenge → Grammar bootcamp p119

Talking about photos

1 Work in pairs. Describe the people in photos 1–3.

2 Watch the video. Who are the people in the photos?

3 Watch again. Which Key phrase do you not hear?

4 Complete the dialogue with the Key phrases. Watch again and check.

Elena: Oh, that's a nice photo. **1** (…) are they?

Owen: That's my grandma and my auntie Sarah.

Elena: **2** (…) are they?

Owen: In my aunt's house.

Elena: That's **3** (…) nice. Have you got any cousins?

Owen: Yes, three. OK, so these are my cousins, Charlie and Johnny.

Elena: Oh – they're twins! That's a **4** (…) photo. Which is Charlie?

Owen: Let's see – **5** (…) is Charlie – he's got blue eyes.

Elena: And **6** (…) this?

Owen: That's their sister Caroline.

Elena: How **7** (…) is she?

Owen: She's 13.

5 Create your own dialogue. Follow the steps in the Skills boost.

SKILLS BOOST

THINK
Find some photos of people you know (family, friends, …).

PREPARE
Prepare a dialogue. Remember to use Key phrases to talk about photos.
Who's that?
These are my friends, Lester and Ollie.

PRACTISE
Practise your dialogue.

PERFORM
Act out your dialogue for the class.

6 **Peer review** Listen to your classmates and answer the questions.

1 Which Key phrases do they use to talk about the people in the photos?
2 Which Key phrases do they use to ask questions?
3 Which Key phrases do they use to give opinions?

Key phrases

Talking about people in a photo:

Who are they?	This is (my auntie).
Who's this/that?	That's (their sister).
Which is (Charlie)?	These are (my cousins).

Asking about a photo:

Where are they?	How old is she?

Giving an opinion about a photo:

That's a great photo.	That's really nice.
That's very funny.	

Real-world grammar

He's got blue eyes.
These are my cousins, Charlie and Johnny.

To: Granddad Monday

Hi Granddad!

How are you? I hope you're well.

I want to ask you a favour. My friend from Manchester, Ben, is here this weekend. Ben's parents are away in Paris for two days. I've got a small problem. I'm busy on Friday evening; I've got basketball practice from 5:00 pm to 7:00 pm. Are you free to meet him at the station? His train is at 6:35 pm.

Ben's 13, too. He isn't very tall. He's got short, black hair and glasses.

I hope this is OK. Thanks, Granddad. See you about 7:15 pm on Friday.

Joshua

An email

1 Read the email from Joshua to his grandfather. Choose the correct description.

- **a** Joshua tells his grandfather about his plans for the weekend.
- **b** Joshua asks his grandfather to help him.
- **c** Joshua tells his grandfather about a new friend.

2 Read the email again and put the paragraphs in the correct order.

- **a** Joshua thanks his grandfather.
- **b** Joshua describes Ben.
- **c** Joshua says 'hello' and asks how his grandfather is.
- **d** Joshua signs his name.
- **e** Joshua describes the problem.

3 Read the email again and correct the sentences.

1. Ben is from London.
2. Ben's parents are in Berlin this weekend.
3. Ben's train is at 5:35 pm.
4. Joshua's got basketball practice from 6:00 to 8:00 pm.
5. Ben's got curly, fair hair.

▶ Subskill: Apostrophes

We use apostrophes to show possession:

This is John's phone.

We also use them to show a letter is missing, e.g. in a contracted form:

He's (He is) a doctor. He's got (He has got) a blue car.

4 Find all the examples with apostrophes in the email. Which example shows possession?

5 Write the contracted forms in the email as full forms.

Writing competence → Workbook pp110–111

6 **Write the sentences with contracted forms.**

1 She is 14.
2 Do not talk.
3 I have got two cousins.
4 They are not English.
5 He has not got brown eyes.
6 It is Monday.
7 I am not her sister.
8 He is not a teacher.
9 You are not in this class.
10 We are from Istanbul.

7 **Write an email to a friend or someone in your family, asking them to meet someone for you. Follow the steps in the Skills boost.**

SKILLS BOOST

THINK

Decide:

- who to write to
- your problem – why are you busy?

PREPARE

1 Write a short description of your friend.
2 Plan your email. Decide what to put in each paragraph. Use the email in exercise 1 to help you.

WRITE

Write your email.

Hi …,

How are you? …

CHECK

Read your email. Check that it includes:

- a description of your problem
- a description of your friend
- words with apostrophes to show possession and contracted forms
- *have got*

8 **Peer review** **Exchange your email with another student. Answer the questions.**

1 Is *have got* correct?
2 Are the apostrophes correct?
3 Is the problem clear?
4 Is there a description of the friend?

Grammar

have got

Affirmative

I/You/We/They've got (have got) two sisters.
He/She/It's got (has got) a brother.

Negative

I/You/We/They haven't got (have not got) black hair.
He/She/It hasn't got (has not got) green eyes.

Questions and short answers

Have I/you/we/they got any cousins?
Yes, I/you/we/they have.
No, I/you/we/they haven't.
Has he/she/it got brown eyes?
Yes, he/she/it has.
No, he/she/it hasn't.

Possessive *'s*

Use *'s* to show possession.
*This is **Julia's** bag.* *That is my **father's** phone.*
Write the apostrophe after a plural noun ending in *-s*.
*This is my **brothers'** room. (more than one brother)*
Write *'s* before a plural noun not ending in *-s*.
*This is the **children's** mother. (more than one child)*

Vocabulary

20 Family

aunt, brother, child/children, cousin, daughter, father, granddaughter, grandfather, grandmother, grandson, mother, nephew, niece, parents, sister, son, uncle

21 Describing people

fair/dark, old/young, tall/short

22 Parts of the body and face

arm, beard, ear, eye, foot/feet, hair, hand, head, leg, moustache, mouth, nose, teeth

23 Describing hair

long/short, curly/straight

2 Project

WDYT? (What do you think?)

What is a family?

TASK: Make a circle map of important people in your life.

Learning outcomes

1 I can describe important people in my life.
2 I can think about things in different ways.
3 I can use appropriate language from the unit.

Graphic organiser → Project planner p130

1 Watch a video of a student presenting his circle map. Who are the people in the map?

STEP 1: THINK

2 Look at the circle map in the Model project. Answer the questions.

1 Who is in the centre of the map?
2 Which family members are included?
3 Who else is included? Why?

3 What can you see in the circle map?

- the names and ages of the people
- photos of the people
- who they are (family, friends, etc.)
- physical descriptions

STEP 2: PLAN

4 Work individually. Make a list of important people in your life.

5 Work in pairs. Read the tips in the Super skills box and practise saying the Key phrases with a partner.

CRITICAL THINKING — SUPER SKILLS

Thinking about things in different ways

Tips

Don't choose your first idea. Write it down, but think about other people too.

Ask: 'Is this true for me?'

Think about why they are important to you (you see them often, you talk about things together, they help you, etc.)

Key phrases

What do you think?
Are other people important?
What about your classmates?
Have you got any cousins/uncles/aunts ... ?
Is/Are your ... important to you?
Are you sure about that?

6 Discuss your list with your partner. Choose the people you want to include in your circle map and where to put them. Use the tips and Key phrases in the Super skills box.

STEP 3: CREATE

7 Make your circle map.

1 Draw five circles. Colour the circles as in the Model project.
2 Write the names of the people in the circles.
3 Add photos and descriptions to your map.

STEP 4: PRESENT

8 Read the *How to ...* tips on p130. Then work in groups of four. Take turns to present your circle map to the group.

Grammar and Vocabulary → Quick review p33

Model project

Circle map

The people in the **orange circle** are the most important.
The people in the **blue circle** are less important.

Ömer and Matthew

Ömer and Matthew are my best friends. We go to school together. Ömer's 13 and Matthew's 12. Ömer's dark, but Matthew's short and fair.

Mum

My mum is very important to me. She's got brown hair and blue eyes, like me.

Ethan

My cousin Ethan is a good friend. He's 12 years old. He's got fair hair and blue eyes. We play video games together.

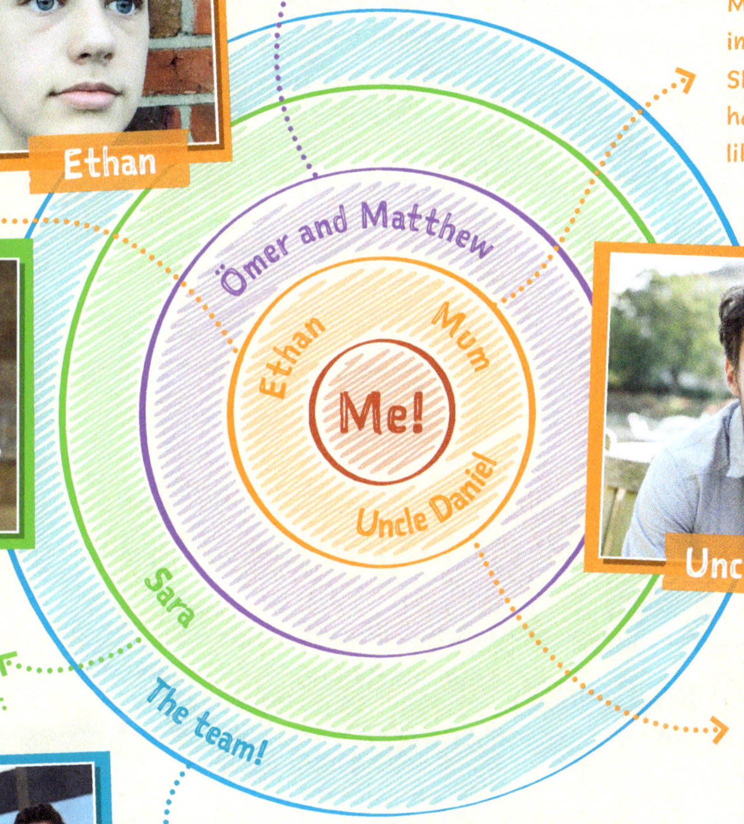

Sara

Sara is my guitar teacher. I love music and I play the bass guitar. Sara's got big blue eyes and long curly hair.

Uncle Daniel

I really like my uncle Daniel. He's my mum's brother. He's tall and dark and he's got a beard.

The team!

My basketball team! We're all different, but we all love basketball!

9 **Peer review** **As you listen to your classmates, answer the questions.**

1 Who are the people in the map?
2 Is their map similar or different to your map? Why?

2 FINAL REFLECTION

1 The task

Do you say who the important people are for you (mum, friend, etc.) and give their names?

Do you describe the people?

2 Super skill

Do you think about things in different ways? Give examples.

3 Language

Do you use language from the unit? Give examples.

3 Eat well

WDYT? (What do you think?)

What's the ideal meal?

Vocabulary: food and drink; the shopping centre

Grammar: countable and uncountable nouns; *some*, *any*, *a lot of*; *there is/are*

Reading: a news story article about Meatless Mondays

Listening: a street interview about shopping centres

Speaking: ordering food

Writing: a blog post about food

Project: plan your ideal meal

Video skills p37

Real-world speaking p43

Project pp46–47

PIZZA QUIZ

1 Do you like pizza?
a I love it! b It's OK. c I don't like it.

2 I eat pizza ...
a every week b every month c on my birthday

3 Where do you eat pizza?
a at home b in a restaurant c in the street

4 I eat pizza ...
a with my family b with friends c alone

Food and drink

1 Work in pairs. Do the quiz. Then compare your answers with your partner.

2 Look at the words in the box. Which are the two typical ingredients for a pizza topping?

banana bread cheese chocolate coffee fish potato tomato water

3 Look at the photos. What are the ingredients on each pizza?

4 24 Listen and check your answers in exercise 3. Note the country where people eat pizzas A–D.

Plurals

Remember, most nouns add *-s* to make the plural, but nouns ending *-s*, *-sh*, *-ch* and *-x* add *-es*. *Tomato* and *potato* also add *-es*.

5 Match the words in the box with photos 1–12.

apple	biscuit	chicken	juice	meat	oil
orange	peas	rice	sandwich	soup	tea

1  2  3  4 

5  6  7  8 

9 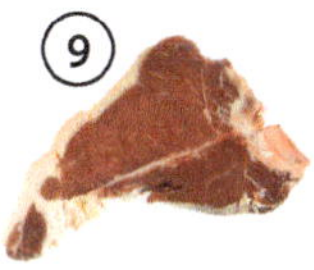 10  11  12 

6 **Work in pairs. Do the three-minute challenge! Read the clues and find the words in exercise 5. Which word is missing?**

1 Some people like coffee. Others prefer this drink.
2 This is good to eat on a cold day or if you are ill.
3 This is food and also the name of an animal.
4 This is red, yellow or green.
5 You can make this from bread, cheese and tomatoes.
6 The name of this fruit is the same as its colour.
7 Vegetarians don't eat this.
8 This is very popular in countries like Japan and China.
9 These are small, round and green.
10 You use this for cooking and in salads.
11 You can make this from oranges.

7 **Look at exercises 2 and 5 again. Find:**

1  four drinks

2  two vegetables

3  three fruits

4  two sweet things

VIDEO SKILLS

8 **Watch the video. What food does Bokang eat?**

9 **Work in pairs. Answer the questions.**

1 Do you think Bokang likes food? Why?
2 Which adjectives describe Bokang: fun, sad, bored or happy?
3 Do you think videos about food are interesting? Why?

Pronunciation: Silent letters → p128

Vocabulary extension → Workbook p102

A news story

1 **Work in pairs. What do you eat? Ask and answer questions using the words and expressions in the boxes.**

biscuit bread chicken fish fruit meat rice vegetables

every day every month every week never one or two days a week

OK, what about meat?

I eat meat one or two days a week. And you?

I eat meat every day.

2 **Do you think you eat well? Why/Why not?**

3 **Look at the infographic. Which subject in the box is not included?**

food health meat sport

Subskill: Understanding the general idea

It's not important to understand every word the first time you read. Just try to get a general idea.

4 25 **The news story answers three questions. Read and listen to the article and match paragraphs 1–3 with questions a–c.**

a Why is Meatless Monday a good idea? Paragraph (…)
b Who organises Meatless Monday? Paragraph (…)
c What is Meatless Monday? Paragraph (…)

5 **What does the news story say? Choose the best answer.**

1 What is Meatless Mondays?
  a a day when people don't eat meat or fish
  b a special day for vegetarians
2 Why is Meatless Mondays a good idea?
  a to save water
  b it's good for the planet and for our health
3 Who organises Meatless Mondays?
  a students, their families and friends
  b big organisations and individual people

6 **Match numbers 1–4 with phrases a–d.**

1 375 million **2** 1,600 **3** 40 **4** 5

a litres of water necessary to produce one burger
b countries that have Meatless Mondays
c North Vancouver schools where students don't eat meat on Mondays
d vegetarians in the world

7 **Word work** **Match the definitions to the words in bold in the text.**

1 for example, Earth, Mars, Venus …
2 the opposite of 'more'
3 the process of making something
4 say you will definitely do or not do something
5 the natural world: land, water, plants and animals
6 for example, oxygen, hydrogen …

8 **The words in bold are in the wrong sentence. Write the sentences with the correct option.**

1 I **production** to be home at 8:00 pm.
2 People in the Netherlands drink **planet** tea than people in Morocco.
3 We write the **environment** 'carbon dioxide' like this: CO_2.
4 Our **promise** is blue because 70% of it is water.
5 China is number 1 for the **less** of mobile phones.
6 Joe's interested in the **gas** and he's got a lot of books about plants and animals.

CRITICAL THINKING

SUPER SKILLS

1 **Remember** What are the reasons in the text for eating a vegetarian diet?
2 **Apply** Can you think of any good reasons for eating meat?
3 **Analyse** Can you think of any other reasons why people don't eat a type of food?

fun facts

Vegetarians don't eat meat. Pescatarians eat fish, but don't eat meat. Vegans don't eat meat, fish or any food from animals.

MEATLESS MONDAYS

1 Today, 375 million people are vegetarian: they don't eat any meat or fish. And a lot of people eat **less** meat because of Meatless Mondays – this means that people **promise** not to eat meat or fish one day a week. But why is it a good thing?

2 Meatless Mondays help people think about the **planet** and their diet. Meat **production** is bad for the **environment**. For example, farm animals produce more **gas** than all the cars and planes in the world. And did you know that you need 1,600 litres of water to produce one burger? Also, a diet with a lot of meat is not good for your body. Some people think a diet with more vegetables and some fruit is a very good idea.

3 Meatless Mondays are now popular in 40 countries. A lot of schools, universities, hospitals and even cities have Meatless Mondays. The idea to have one day without meat every week often starts with just one individual. Vancouver student Meghan Little is a vegan: she doesn't eat any food from animals. This includes milk and cheese. Because of Meghan's work, Mondays are now meat-free at her school and four other schools in North Vancouver. With Meatless Mondays, one person can make a big difference to the lives of their family and friends, and to the planet.

Cows, sheep and other farm animals produce more gas than all the cars and planes in the world.

Fruit and vegetables are good for your heart.

Meat production uses 33% of the planet's land.

3,500 **schools, hospitals and restaurants in the USA have Meatless Mondays.**

The longer read → Resource centre

Countable and uncountable nouns

Some nouns are countable: we can count 1, 2, 3 apples.
Some nouns are uncountable: we can't count meat.

1 Put the words in the box into two groups, countable and uncountable.

banana biscuit bread cheese coffee
juice orange potato soup tea

2 Read what Jake says. Which things in his packed lunch are uncountable?

I've got two **sandwiches**, some **tomatoes**, a **biscuit**, some **juice**, **water** and an **apple**.

3 Choose the correct option to complete the rules.

1 We use *a* or *an* with singular **countable/uncountable** nouns.
2 **Countable/Uncountable** nouns haven't got a plural form.
3 We **can/can't** use *some* or nothing with uncountable nouns.
4 We can use *some* or a number with **plural countable/uncountable** nouns.

4 Correct the sentences.

1 I've got breads and a cheese.
I've got some bread and some cheese.
2 Kelly's got two banana and a water.
3 Jesse's got a apple and sandwich.
4 Lee's got an biscuit and juices.

some, any, a lot of

5 Read the examples. Match sentence halves 1–4 with a–d to make rules.

A lot of schools have Meatless Mondays.
It isn't good to eat a lot of meat.
Meghan doesn't eat any food from animals.
We haven't got any tomatoes.
We've got some cheese and some oranges.
Have you got any bread?

1 We use *some*, *any* and *a lot of* with
2 *A lot of* describes
3 *Some* describes
4 We use *any* in

a negative sentences and questions.
b both countable and uncountable nouns.
c a big number or amount.
d a number or amount that is not big or small.

6 Choose the correct option.

1 Sorry, I haven't got **any/some** coffee.
2 I've got **any/some** free time today. I can help you.
3 Have you got **any/some** sisters?
4 English, history, maths, Spanish, biology … I've got **some/a lot of** homework tonight!
5 She's got **a lot of/any** cousins, but she hasn't got **some/any** brothers and sisters.

7 Complete the text with *some*, *any* or *a lot of*. Use the percentages (%) to help you.

1 (75%) *A lot of* children in the UK have a packed lunch, but is their lunch healthy? **2 (41%)** (…) children don't eat **3 (0%)** (…) vegetables and **4 (47%)** (…) parents give their children cake or chocolate in their lunchbox. Have they got **5 (?%)** (…) fruit in their lunchboxes? For 10% of children in the UK, the answer is no. They don't eat **6 (0%)** (…) fruit. And in the USA, **7 (33%)** (…) parents think juice is a healthy drink, but it's got a lot of sugar.

8 Answer the question to solve the Brain teaser.

BRAIN TEASER

Alex, Ben and Carla have each got a different drink: tea, water or juice, and a different type of fruit: apple, orange or banana.

Alex has got an orange, but she hasn't got any tea.
Ben has got some tea and an apple.
Carla hasn't got any juice.

Which drink and fruit has each person got?

Reinforcement and Challenge → Grammar bootcamp pp119–120

The shopping centre

1 **Look at the map of a shopping centre. Match numbers 1–5 with the places in the box.**

baker's café food stall restaurant supermarket

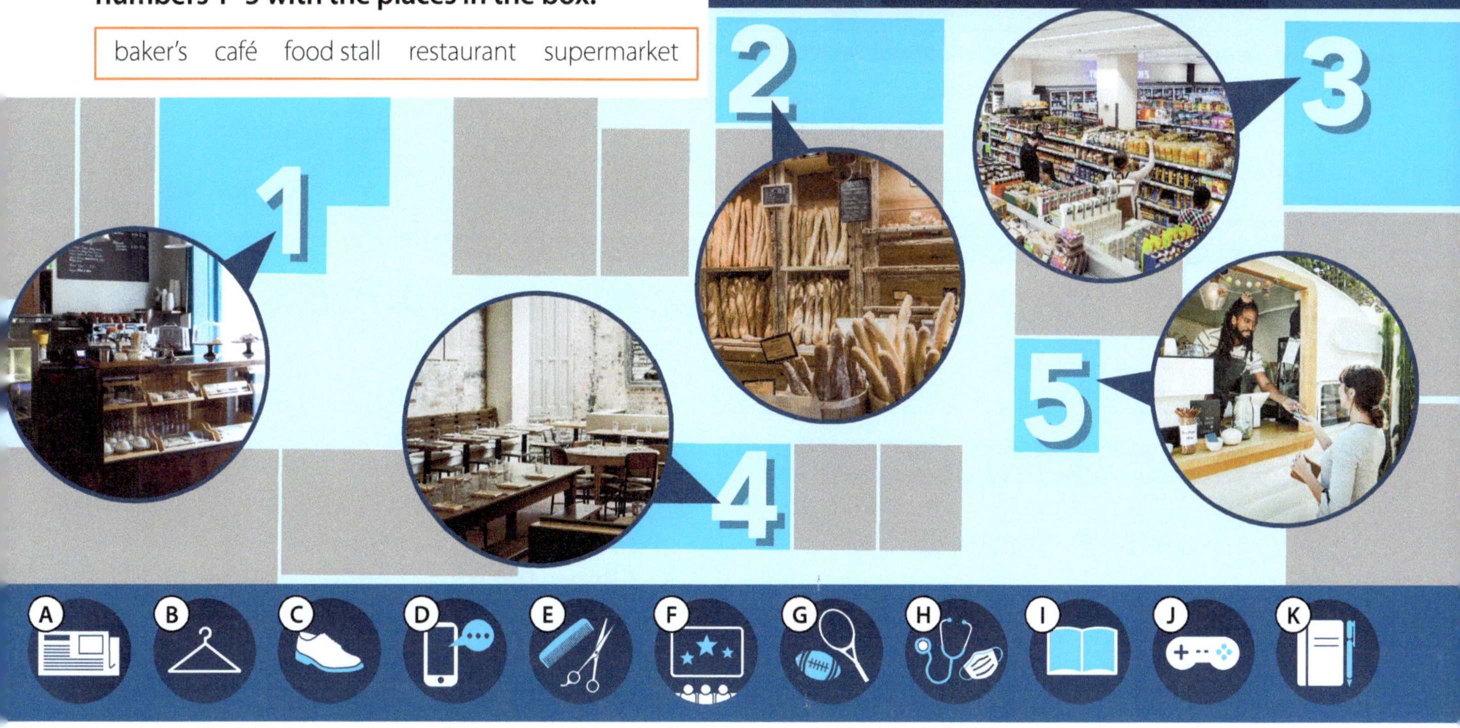

2 **Work in pairs. What's your favourite place to buy food in a shopping centre? Why?**

3 **Match icons A–K with the words in the box.**

bookshop chemist's cinema clothes shop games shop hairdresser's newsagent's phone shop shoe shop sports shop stationery shop

Possessive 's in shops

We use a possessive *'s* for some shops, e.g. *baker's*, *chemist's*. They are the baker's (shop), the chemist's (shop).

4 **Where can you buy the things on the shopping list? (More than one answer is possible.)**

1 pens and a notebook
2 bread and biscuits
3 popcorn
4 medicine, aspirin
5 comics
6 tennis balls

A street interview

5 26 **Listen to a street interview. Number questions a–d in the order you hear them.**

a Is there a shopping centre in your town?
b What's good about it?
c What's your favourite place to go shopping?
d Are there other things to do at the shopping centre?

Subskill: Taking notes while you listen

When you listen, write short notes. Don't try to write complete sentences.

6 **Listen again. Copy the table and make notes.**

	Westfield Centre	Mall of America
Types of shops		
Places to eat and drink		
Other things to do		

7 **Work in pairs. Ask and answer the questions in exercise 5.**

What's your favourite place to go shopping?

My favourite place is Xanadú, near Madrid. It's got …

there is/are

1 Read the examples. Copy and complete the tables.

Is there a shopping centre in your town? Yes, there is.
There aren't any shops where I live.
There's a cinema. There are some cafés and food stalls.
Are there any other things to do? Yes, there are.

	Affirmative	Negative
Singular	**1** (…) a cinema.	There isn't an aquarium.
Plural	**2** (…) some cafés and food stalls.	**3** (…) any shops where I live.

	Question	Short answers
Singular	**4** (…) a shopping centre in your town?	Yes, **5** (…) ./No, there isn't.
Plural	**6** (…) any other things to do?	Yes, there are./No, there aren't.

2 Choose the correct option.

1 There **is/are** two cinemas in my town.
2 There **is/are** a stationery shop.
3 There **is/are** a good bookshop.
4 There **is/are** some cheap restaurants.
5 There **is/are** three sports shops.

3 Read the web page. Complete the sentences with *There's*, *There isn't*, *There are* or *There aren't*.

Visit **LEE SHOPPING CENTRE**

- 10 clothes shops
- 8 shoe shops
- 3 restaurants
- 2 bookshops
- 5 cafés
- 1 phone shop

Plus a supermarket, a hairdresser's and a cinema!

1 (…) a games shop.
2 (…) some shoe shops.
3 (…) a phone shop.
4 (…) any food stalls.
5 (…) a chemist's.

4 Order the words to make questions. Then write short answers with the information in exercise 3.

1 is / baker's / there / a ?
2 cafés / any / there / are ?
3 any / there / are / sports shops ?
4 supermarket / there / a / is ?
5 a newsagent's / there / is ?

5 Complete the dialogue with the correct form of *there is/are*.

1 (…) any good places to eat where you live?

Yes, **2** (…) . **3** (…) a good pizza restaurant near my home.

4 (…) a Japanese restaurant?

No, **5** (…) , but **6** (…) an Indian restaurant. What about where you live?

6 Work in pairs. Ask about places near your partner's home.

Are there any cafés near your home?

Yes, there are. There are a lot. Is there a games shop near you?

7 Choose the correct option.

GRAMMAR ROUND-UP

1 2 3 4 5 6 7 8

Hong Kong's unusual cafés

News About Reviews Search

There are a lot of good places to eat in Hong Kong. There are **1 a/some** unusual cafés, too! Our favourite **2 is/are** the Duck Café. This place **3 have got/has got** ducks in all its food! And **4 there's/there are** a café with a *Harry Potter* theme. The **5 café's/cafés'** name is 9¾ Café, and there are things from the *Harry Potter* films on the walls.

These cafés **6 isn't/aren't** only for eating and drinking. There are things to do, too. For example, two cafés **7 have got/has got** go-karts!

It's all very strange! Are there **8 some/any** unusual cafés where you live?

Research

Find out if there are any unusual cafés where you live.

Reinforcement and Challenge → Grammar bootcamp p120

Ordering food

1 Read the menu. What type of food is there?

2 Watch the video. Write the food and drink in Connor's order.

3 Watch again. Which Key phrase is not in the conversation?

4 Complete the dialogue with the Key phrases. Watch again and check.

Server: Hi.

Connor: Hi. **1** (…) a veggie burger, please?

Server: One vegetarian burger. **2** (…) any fries with that?

Connor: Yes, please, some cheese fries.

Server: **3** Would you like (…) to drink?

Connor: Do you have any juice?

Server: No, I'm sorry, we don't.

Connor: OK, **4** (…) a bottle of water, please.

Server: Anything **5** (…) ?

Connor: What do you have for dessert?

Server: We have cheesecake, cupcakes …

Connor: A chocolate cupcake, please. **6** (…) is that?

Server: That's $9.25, please.

Connor: Here you go. Thanks!

Burgers

Cheeseburger	$5.50
Veggie burger	$4.00
Burger special	$6.00

Sides

Fries	$2.70
Cheese fries	$3.00
Green salad	$1.80

Desserts

Fruit salad	$2.50
Cupcake	$1.50
Cheesecake	$1.75
Apple pie	$2.00

Drinks

Coffee	$1.20
Tea	$1.00
Banana smoothie	$1.10
Bottle of water	$0.75

5 Create your own dialogue. Follow the steps in the Skills boost.

SKILLS BOOST

THINK
Choose food and drink from the menu in exercise 1 (or create your own menu).

PREPARE
Prepare a dialogue. Use Key phrases for ordering food.
Hi.
Hi. Can I have …

PRACTISE
Practise your dialogue. Take turns to be the customer.

PERFORM
Act out your dialogue for the class.

6 **Peer review** Listen to your classmates and answer the questions.

1 What is the order? (food and drink)
2 What is the total cost of the order?
3 Are the Key phrases correct?

Key phrases

Can I have a/some … , please?
I'd like a/some … , please.
Would you like any … with that?
Would you like anything to drink?
Anything else?
That's all, thanks.
How much is that?
That's … , please.

US → UK

Would you like any fries with that? (US) → Would you like any chips with that? (UK)

HOME POSTS PHOTOS RECIPES

Brazil is a big country. The food is different in different regions, but these are some typical dishes.

a Feijoada

Meat is important in Brazilian cooking. This is a meat stew with beans. It's delicious, but it takes 24 hours to cook. Most people eat it in restaurants.

b Moqueca

This fish stew is popular in the north of the country. You cook fish with tomatoes, onions and coconut milk and you serve it with rice.

c Empadão

Empadão is a famous Brazilian pie. It is a typical meal for lunch and dinner at the weekend. There are different types of pie, but the most common is with meat or fish.

d Pão de queijo

This is a type of bread. You make balls with bread and cheese and you eat them for breakfast or as a snack during the day.

A blog post about food

1 **Work in pairs. What country are the dishes in the box from?**

curry kebab paella sushi tacos

People eat tacos in the USA.

Yes, but they're from …

2 Read the blog post. Choose a title.

a Food around the world
b My favourite dishes
c Food in my country

3 Read the blog post again. Match photos 1–4 with descriptions a–d.

4 Answer the questions.

1 What are the ingredients in the four dishes?
Feijoada – meat and …
2 Where is it typical to eat feijoada? Why?
3 Where is moqueca from?
4 When is it usual to eat empadão and pão de queijo?

Subskill: *and* and *but*

We use *and* and *but* to connect ideas in a sentence.

5 Read the examples. Choose the correct option to complete the rules.

*You make balls with bread **and** cheese.*
*It's delicious, **but** it takes 24 hours to cook.*

1 We use ***and/but*** to add a similar idea.
2 We use ***and/but*** to add a different idea.
3 We often use a comma (,) before ***and/but***.

Writing competence → Workbook pp112–113

6 Find other examples of *and* and *but* in the blog.

7 Complete the sentences with *and* or *but*.

1. You make paella with rice (…) fish.
2. In India, people eat curry for lunch (…) dinner.
3. It's common in the south of the country, (…) not in the north.
4. I like fish, (…) not in sandwiches.
5. Pizza is common in Italy (…) in other countries.
6. I eat a lot of burgers, (…) not with chips.

8 Write a blog post about food in your country. Follow the steps in the Skills boost.

SKILLS BOOST

THINK

Choose four typical dishes in your country.

PREPARE

Make notes about:

- the ingredients in each dish
- where people eat them
- when people eat them
- what you eat them with

WRITE

Write your blog. Use expressions from the model.

… is a type of bread/stew/sandwich/dessert

you cook … with …

you serve it with …

… is a typical meal for breakfast/lunch/dinner

CHECK

Read your blog. Check for:

- *a, an, some, any, a lot of* (+ countable and uncountable nouns)
- *there is/are*
- *and, but*

9 **Peer review** Exchange your blog post with another student. Answer the questions.

1. Is the language correct? (grammar and vocabulary)
2. Is the information correct? (Are they typical dishes? Are the ingredients correct?)
3. With your partner, choose your four favourite.

Grammar

Countable and uncountable nouns

Some nouns are countable. They have a plural form.

apples, chips, potatoes

Some nouns are uncountable. They are never plural.

bread, meat, milk

With countable nouns, we use *a/an*, a number, or *some*.

I've got ***an*** *apple. He's got* ***three*** *apples.*

We've got ***some*** *apples.*

With uncountable nouns, we use *some*.

She's got ***some*** *milk.*

some, any, a lot of

We use *some* and *any* with countable and uncountable nouns.

We use *some* in affirmative sentences.

I've got ***some*** *biscuits. He's got* ***some*** *chocolate.*

We use *any* in negative sentences and questions.

They haven't got ***any*** *peas. They haven't got* ***any*** *soup.*

Have you got ***any*** *biscuits? Have you got* ***any*** *chocolate?*

We use *a lot of* to describe a big number. We use *a lot of* with countable and uncountable nouns.

She's got ***a lot of*** *chips. They eat* ***a lot of*** *ice cream.*

there is/are

We use *there is/are* to say that something exists.

With singular countable nouns and uncountable nouns, we use *there is* (*there's*).

With plural nouns, we use *there are*.

There's *a shopping centre in my town.*

There are *two clothes shops.*

In negative sentences, we use *there isn't/there aren't*.

There isn't *a bookshop.*

There aren't *any shoe shops.*

In questions, we use *Is/Are there?*

Is there *a hairdresser's? Yes,* ***there is****./No,* ***there isn't****.*

Are there *any games shops? Yes,* ***there are****./No,* ***there aren't****.*

We don't use contracted forms in the affirmative short answer.

Yes, there is. NOT ~~*Yes, there's.*~~

Vocabulary

27 Food and drink

apple, banana, biscuit, bread, cheese, chicken, chocolate, coffee, fish, juice, meat, oil, orange, peas, potato, rice, sandwich, soup, tea, tomato, water

28 The shopping centre

baker's, bookshop, café, chemist's, cinema, clothes shop, food stall, games shop, hairdresser's, newsagent's, phone shop, restaurant, shoe shop, sports shop, stationery shop, supermarket

3 Project

WDYT?
(What do you think?)

What's the ideal meal?

TASK: Plan your ideal meal.

Learning outcomes

1 I can plan and present my ideal meal.
2 I can work well with others.
3 I can use appropriate language from the unit.

Graphic organiser → Project planner p131

1 Watch a video of students presenting their ideal meal. Would you like to go to this meal? Why/Why not?

STEP 1: THINK

2 Look at the different headings on the mind map in the Model project. Add the ideas to the correct section.

after school at an Italian restaurant
chocolate fish and salad Friday evening
my American cousin's visit my birthday
my family my grandparents
at a vegetarian café no special reason
people from my class pizza
Sunday lunchtime at home

- Reason for the meal
- What to eat
- Where to eat
- When
- Who to share it with

3 Work in pairs. Add another idea to each part of the mind map.

STEP 2: PLAN

4 Work in pairs. Read the tips in the Super skills box and practise saying the Key phrases with a partner.

COLLABORATION — SUPER SKILLS

Working well together

Tips

Listen to your partner's ideas.
Decide together.
Share the work.

Key phrases

What do you think about … ?
OK, I agree.
That's a good idea.
No, but what about … ?
I've got the photos.
Let's do it this way.
OK, I can type the text.

5 Work in pairs. Make notes about your ideal meal. Use the ideas in exercise 2.

STEP 3: CREATE

6 Read the *How to …* tips on p131 and create your mind map with your notes from exercise 5. Either use an online tool or prepare it by hand. Use the tips and Key phrases in the Super skills box.

7 Think again about your reason for your ideal meal and the people you want to invite. Why do you have these things?

- the place
- the type of food
- the time

Grammar and Vocabulary → Quick review p45

Model project

Celebrate the end of term

Reason for the meal

Our best friends (Tara, Emma, Lucy, Ross and Mark)

Who to share it with

OUR IDEAL MEAL

Sandwiches, cheese, biscuits ...

What to eat

When

Where to eat

Saturday 23rd July (day after school finishes)

Victoria Park

STEP 4: PRESENT

8 Peer review **Work with another pair. In turns, present your mind map and explain your decisions. As you listen to your classmates, answer the questions.**

1 Are the food and the place right for the people?
2 Would you like to go to this meal? Why/Why not?

3 FINAL REFLECTION

1 **The task**
Is the mind map clear and attractive?

2 **Super skill**
How well do you work together? Give examples.

3 **Language**
In your menu and presentation, do you use language from the unit? Give examples.

4 My time

WDYT? (What do you think?)

Why is it a good idea to organise your time?

Vocabulary: the time; daily routines; free-time activities

Grammar: present simple; *love/like/don't like/hate* + noun; object pronouns

Reading: an online article about life in a K-pop academy

Listening: a conversation about a phone app

Speaking: making plans

Writing: notes and messages

Project: make a digital poster story about a typical day

Video skills p49

Real-world speaking p55

Project pp58–59

A DAY IN THE LIFE OF A TEEN AND HIS PHONE

7:15 am: get up

7:45 am: have breakfast

8:35 am: go to school

9:00 am–1:00 pm: have lessons

The time; daily routines

1 Copy the clock and write the phrases in the box in the correct order.

five to	half past	o'clock
quarter to	twenty past	

2 29 Draw six clocks. Listen and write the times on the clocks.

Language note

twelve o'clock = midday or midnight

3 Work in pairs. In turns, draw a clock and ask your partner the time.

What time is it?

It's twenty past ten. What time is it?

Language note

We use digital times in timetables, schedules, etc. We say these as we write them, e.g.

1:30 = one thirty *4:15 = four fifteen*
10:30 = ten thirty *11:45 = eleven forty-five*

4 What time does the boy do the activities in the box?

do homework	get up	go to bed	have lunch

5 Match times 1–3 with other activities a–c in the boy's day.

1	9:00 am	**a**	relax
2	3:30 pm	**b**	finish school
3	8:15–9:55 pm	**c**	start school

6 Read about the boy's day. Correct the phrases in bold.

On a typical school day, I **1 go to bed** at quarter past seven. I **2 have lunch** at about quarter to eight, and then I **3 start school** at twenty-five to nine. I **4 relax** in the morning, and then at about ten past one, I **5 go home**. I **6 have lunch** again in the afternoon, and I **7 do my homework** at five to four. I **8 have lessons** at about half past five. I have dinner with my family at half past seven, and then I **9 finish school**. I **10 get up** at five to ten.

7 Work in pairs. Compare your day and the boy's day. What is the same and what is different?

I get up at seven. That's different.

And I go to school at half past seven.

VIDEO SKILLS

8 Watch the video. What is Lucy's job?

9 Work in pairs. Answer the questions.

1 Why are documentaries about animals popular?
2 Where can you watch documentaries like this?

An online article

1 Work in pairs. Look at the photos on p51 and answer the questions.

WHAT DO YOU KNOW ABOUT K-POP?

1 Where is K-pop from?
2 What type of music is it?
3 What is special about K-pop?
4 What K-pop singers are popular in your country?

2 Read the 'Did you know?' box on p51 and check your answers in exercise 1.

3 Is it easy or difficult to become a K-pop singer? Read the article quickly and find the answer.

Subskill: Reading for detail

When you complete notes about a text, first look at the gaps and the words around them in the exercise. This helps you to read quickly to find the missing information in the text.

4 30 Read and listen to the article. Complete the schedule for a typical day.

MY schedule

5:00 am	**1** (…) , have breakfast	✓
2 (…)	start school	✓
3 (…)	go to practice room	✓
7:00 pm	**4** (…) (singing, dancing, languages)	
5 (…)	finish lessons	
12:00 am	**6** (…)	

5 Are the sentences true or false? Give reasons for your answers.

1 K-pop stars are very popular.
2 The typical K-pop student is 14 years old.
3 Most K-pop students talk to their friends between lessons.
4 They practise before they have dinner.
5 Students from other countries learn English, Chinese and Japanese.
6 They learn foreign languages to speak to people in Korea.

6 Read about Lee Jae-Gi and Jamie Choi. What do they do to become K-pop stars?

7 **Word work** Match the definitions to the words in bold in the text.

1 a famous or popular person
2 good things happening to you by chance
3 a person who likes a type of music or sport very much
4 events when a singer or music group plays in front of people
5 free time between lessons
6 start to be something

8 Complete the sentences with words from exercise 7. Which sentences are true for you?

1 I'm a big (…) of Manchester City.
2 I love music, so I'd love to go to a (…) one day.
3 I want to (…) a teacher in the future.
4 I chat with my friends during the (…) at school.
5 Jennifer Lawrence is my favourite film (…) .
6 I'm (…) because I've got a lot of good friends.

CRITICAL THINKING

SUPER SKILLS

1 **Remember** Think about the article. Why is the life of a K-pop student 'difficult'?
They get up early, …

2 **Apply** How are the lives of these people difficult?
- a teen actor
- a teen Olympic swimmer
- a teen concert musician

3 **Evaluate** What are two advantages and two disadvantages about the type of life in questions 1 and 2? Think about:

friends   hobbies and free time
homework   the future   things they learn

LIFE IN A k-pop academy

K-pop is popular all over the world. K-pop singers and bands like BTS and Chungha have got millions of fans, and many teenagers want to be the next big star. If they're lucky, they go to a special academy in South Korea. They learn to dance and sing – but life for a K-pop academy student isn't easy!

Most students are 8 to 14 years old, so they have normal lessons during the day. They get up early, sometimes at five o'clock, and have breakfast. They start school at eight. They study all day, and they don't relax between lessons. Most students practise, listen to music or write songs during the **breaks**.

They finish school at five o'clock, but they don't go home. They go to the practice rooms until dinner time.

After dinner, at seven o'clock, they have lessons in dancing and singing, and language lessons, too. Korean students learn English, Chinese and Japanese, and students from other countries learn Korean. K-pop stars often travel to other countries for **concerts**, so foreign languages are important.

Lessons finish at ten o'clock, but most students practise for another hour or two. Then they go home. They usually go to bed after midnight, and the next day, they start again!

Lee Jae-Gi is from Seoul. He doesn't relax after school. He studies K-pop, hip hop and singing for three hours every evening. He wants to go to a K-pop academy in the future.

Jamie Choi goes to a K-pop school in New York. She also makes music videos and puts them on the internet. She'd like to **become** a K-pop star one day.

Did you know?

K-pop, or Korean pop, is a type of music from South Korea. The music is a mix of different musical styles, including rock, pop, hip hop and jazz. K-pop stars dance and sing at the same time. They are also famous for their music videos.

Present simple: affirmative

1 Read the examples. Copy and complete the rules with the phrases in the box.

They get up early.
I start school at eight o'clock.
She makes music videos.
He wants to go to a K-pop academy.

-s to most verbs routines and facts the infinitive

1 We use the present simple to talk about (…) .
2 With *I/you/we/they*, we use the same form as (…) .
3 With *he/she/it*, we add (…) .

2 Read spelling rules a–c. Write the third person singular form of the verbs in the box.

do finish go have relax study

a We add *-es* to verbs that end in *-s*, *-o*, *-ch*, *-sh* and *-x*.
b For verbs that end in consonant + *-y*, omit the *-y* and add *-ies*.
c Some verbs have an irregular form.

3 Choose the correct option.

1 My brother **do/does** his homework after dinner.
2 I **get up/gets up** late on Saturdays.
3 We **finish/finishes** school early on Wednesdays.
4 My cousin **study/studies** Japanese.
5 My sister **have/has** singing lessons.
6 Jack and I **go/goes** home for lunch.

Present simple: negative

4 Read the examples. Choose the correct option to complete the rules.

They don't go home at five o'clock.
He doesn't relax after school.
I don't write songs in the breaks.
She doesn't live in South Korea.

1 After *I/you/we/they*, we use ***don't/doesn't*** + infinitive without *to*.
2 After *he/she/it*, we use ***don't/doesn't*** + infinitive without *to*.

5 Change the sentences from affirmative to negative, or negative to affirmative.

1 I do my homework before dinner.
I don't do my homework before dinner.
2 My mum speaks Chinese.
3 My friends and I don't relax at the weekend.
4 My dad doesn't work on Saturdays.
5 I get up early on Sundays.
6 Our teacher doesn't have lunch at school.
7 My friend doesn't go to bed at midnight.

6 Work in pairs. Which sentences in exercise 5 are true for you?

I don't do my homework before dinner. I relax after school.

Really? I do my homework before dinner.

7 Complete the article with the present simple form of the verbs.

SCHOOLNEWS NEWS ABOUT STORIES

A DAY IN THE LIFE OF A SAXOPHONE PLAYER

Ethan Williams **1** (…) **(get up)** early every day, and he **2** (…) **(go)** to school at twenty to seven. His lessons **3** (…) **(not start)** then. He usually **4** (…) **(spend)** an hour in the music room. He **5** (…) **(have)** lessons in the morning and again after lunch, but he **6** (…) **(not go)** home at the end of the school day. He **7** (…) **(practise)** in the music room for another two hours. Then he **8** (…) **(study)** the saxophone with a private teacher for an hour. After the lesson, he and his family **9** (…) **(have)** dinner, and **10** he (…) **(play)** the saxophone again before bedtime!

8 Answer the question to solve the Brain teaser.

BRAIN TEASER

Lana, Juliet and Grace are sisters.
Lana starts school half an hour before her sister Grace.
Grace starts school a quarter of an hour after Juliet.
Juliet has lessons from 8:45 am to 3:30 pm.
The school day for each sister is the same.

What time do Lana and Grace finish school?

Reinforcement and Challenge → Grammar bootcamp pp120–121
Pronunciation: Pronouncing *-es* /ɪz/ → p128

Free-time activities

1 **Work in pairs. Discuss the questions.**

1. Which apps are popular in your country?
2. What different types of apps do you and your friends use? (games, social media, music)

2 **Look at the mobile phone. Match icons 1–16 with the activities in the box.**

chat on my phone   do sport   go out on my bike   go shopping   go swimming   go to the cinema   listen to music   meet friends   play basketball   play the guitar   play the piano   play video games   read   sleep   take photos   watch TV

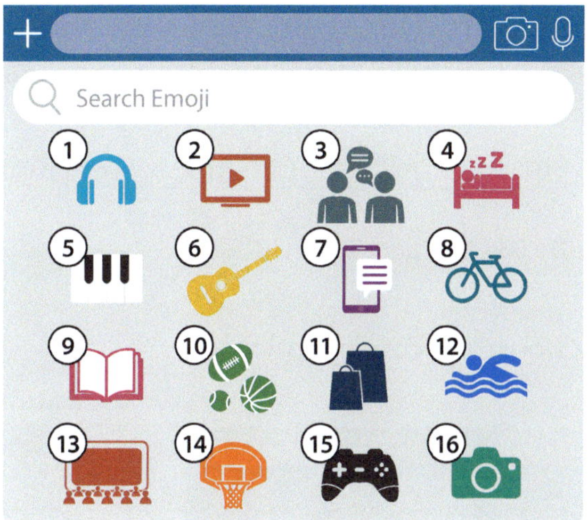

3 **Write out the text conversations. Replace the app icons with some of the activities in exercise 2.**

Conversation 1

Rhona

Alfie: Are you free this afternoon? Why don't we **1** [icon] or **2** [icon] ?

Rhona: I haven't got any money. Come to my house and we can **3** [icon] and **4** [icon] .

Alfie: OK.

Conversation 2

Carl

Angus: Hi. Are you free to **5** [icon] this weekend?

Carl: Yes, good idea. Why don't we **6** [icon] ?

Angus: It's too hot. Let's **7** [icon] .

4 **Where do you usually do the activities in exercise 2? Copy and complete the table.**

At home	Not at home	Both

A conversation

5 **Work in pairs. Look at a page from an app. What's it for?**

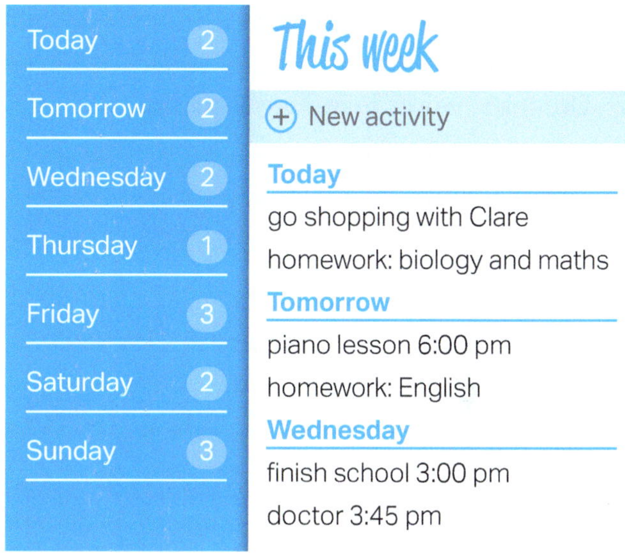

6 31 **Listen to a conversation about the app.**

1. Check your answer in exercise 5.
2. Are the people friends or a teacher and a student?

Subskill: Listening to complete sentences

Listen for the words in the first part of the sentence so you know when the answer is coming.

7 **Listen again. Complete the sentences.**

1. On Thursdays, Flora goes (…) .
2. Flora doesn't know what activity she has got this (…) .
3. Ross has got a new app. It helps him organise his (…) .
4. On the left, you've got the days of the (…) .
5. On Tuesday 10th February, Ross plans to play basketball with (…) .

8 **Work in pairs. Discuss the questions.**

1. Do you think an organising app is a good idea?
2. How do you organise your studies and activities?

Research

Find an organising app for students that you would like to try.

Present simple: *Yes/No* questions and short answers

1 **Copy and complete the tables with the words in the box.**

do Does doesn't use Yes,

Yes/No questions			Short answers
Do/Does	**subject**	**verb?**	Yes, I **3** (…) .
Do	you	**1** (…) it a lot?	No, I don't.
2 (…)	it	help?	**4** (…) it does.
			No, it **5** (…) .

2 **Order the words to make questions.**

1. do / sport / do / you ?
2. your mother / does / English / speak ?
3. have breakfast / at school / you / do ?
4. best friend / does / play the guitar / your ?

3 **Answer the questions in exercise 2 for you.**

Present simple: *Wh-* questions

4 **Look at the examples in the table. Then write questions for the answers.**

Question word	*do/does*	subject	verb?
What time	do	they	get up?
How	does	it	work?
Where	do	you	add activities?

1. What time *do you get up?* I get up at seven o'clock.
2. How (…) She goes to school by car.
3. Where (…) I have lunch at school.
4. What time (…) We finish school at three o'clock.

5 **Work in pairs. Ask and answer the questions in exercise 4 for you.**

love/ like/ don't like/ hate + noun

6 **Copy and complete the sentences with *love* (♥♥), *like* (♥), *don't like* (✗) or *hate* (✗✗).**

1. She / pizza **(♥♥)** *She loves pizza.*
2. He / football **(✗)**
3. We / the cinema **(♥)**
4. She / basketball **(✗✗)**
5. You / Chinese food **(✗)**
6. I / burgers **(♥♥)**

Object pronouns

7 **Read the examples. Then match subject pronouns 1–7 with the object pronouns in the box.**

Our new Spanish teacher is nice – I like her. I've got two new video games. I love them.

her him it ~~me~~ them us you

1. I *me*
2. you (singular and plural)
3. he
4. she
5. it
6. we
7. they

8 **Work in pairs. Ask and answer about the people and things in the box.**

basketball Bruno Mars Maisie Williams sports the cinema vegetables

Do you like sports?

I love them!

9 **Choose the correct option.**

GRAMMAR ROUND-UP

1 2 3 4 **5 6 7 8**

JOE: What's this sport in the photo? **1 It is/ Is it** table tennis?

BETH: No, it **2 isn't/aren't**. It's Teqball. **3 Some/Any** international footballers, like Dani Alves and Neymar, play Teqball and they love **4 him/it**! Neymar **5 has got/have got** a Teqball table in his house and **6 there is/there are** videos of him playing Teqball on YouTube!

JOE: But I **7 don't know/know not** anything about Teqball. How much **8 do cost it/does it cost**?

BETH: The special table costs a lot of money: $3,000!

Reinforcement and Challenge → Grammar bootcamp pp121–122

Making plans

1 Work in pairs. Look at photos 1–3. What can you see?

2 Watch the video. Which activity do the friends decide to do, and when?

3 Watch again. Number the Key phrases in the order you hear them.

4 Complete the dialogue with the Key phrases. Watch again and check.

Amy: Hi Owen.

Owen: Hey Amy, how are you?

Amy: I'm fine. You?

Owen: I'm good.

Amy: Listen, are you **1** (…) on Saturday?

Owen: Sorry, I'm **2** (…) . It's my mum's birthday.

Amy: What **3** (…) Sunday?

Owen: Sunday's **4** (…) . What do you want to do?

Amy: I've got a new video game. Do you want to come and play it?

Owen: Yes, **5** (…) . Is 10:00 **6** (…) ?

Amy: Well, I get up late on Sundays. Why **7** (…) we meet at 11:30?

Owen: OK, **8** (…) . See you on Sunday at half past eleven.

Amy: See you, bye.

1

2

3

5 Create your own dialogue. Follow the steps in the Skills boost.

SKILLS BOOST

THINK
Write a list of free-time activities.

PREPARE
Prepare a dialogue between two friends making plans. Remember to include Key phrases.
Hi Lucía. How are you?
I'm fine.
Are you free on Friday evening?

PRACTISE
Practise your dialogue.

PERFORM
Act out your dialogue for the class.

6 **Peer review** Listen to your classmates and answer the questions.

1. What do they decide to do and when?
2. Which Key phrases do they use for making suggestions and saying *Yes* or *No*?
3. Would you like to do this activity with them? Why/Why not?

Key phrases

Making suggestions	**Saying *Yes* or *No***
Why don't we (meet)?	(Sunday)'s good.
Are you free on (Saturday)?	OK, fine.
What about (Sunday/11:30)?	Yes, great.
Is (Sunday/10:00) OK?	Sorry, I'm busy.

Real-world grammar

What do you want to do?
Do you want to come and play it?
I get up late on Sundays.

MY NOTES

1

Hi Bella,
It's Sam's birthday on Sunday. Do you want to get a present together because I haven't got a lot of money?
(...)

A

Hello Polly,
That's fine. Please order it because I've got a meeting this evening.
Thanks,
(...)

2

Hi Luca,
Remember to come home early today because you've got a maths exam tomorrow.
(...)

B

Hi Dad,
OK, fine. See you at 5:30.
Have you got time to help me study?
(...)

3

Hi Mum,
Please don't buy burgers for tonight because Fatima doesn't eat meat – she's a vegetarian. Pizza?
See you later!
(...)

C

Dear Clare,
Great idea. Why don't we go shopping after school? Have you got any ideas?
(...)

Notes and messages

1 **Read messages 1–3 and match them with replies A–C. Then complete them with the missing names.**

2 **Read the notes and messages again and answer the questions.**

Who … ?

1 doesn't eat meat
2 has got a meeting this evening
3 has got a maths exam tomorrow
4 has got a birthday at the weekend
5 hasn't got a lot of money

3 **Find three ways to start a message and two ways to finish it.**

▶ Subskill: *because*

We use *because* when we give a reason.

4 **Find four sentences with *because* in the messages.**

5 **Choose the correct option to complete the rules.**

1 The reason comes **before/after** *because*.
2 After *because* we write **subject + verb/verb + subject**.

6 **Rewrite the sentences with *because* in the correct position.**

1 This isn't my English book my book is green.
2 I'm sorry. I don't eat chicken I'm a vegetarian.
3 Rory isn't in school today he's ill.
4 I'm not free today it's my grandmother's birthday.

Writing competence → Workbook pp114–115

7 **Complete the sentences with your own reasons.**

1 Remember to come home early because …
2 I'm not free on Sunday because …
3 I want to go to the city centre at the weekend because …
4 Don't forget to call Maria because …

8 **Write two messages. Follow the steps in the Skills boost.**

SKILLS BOOST

THINK

1 Work in pairs. Look at the sentences in exercise 7. Choose two sentences and include one in each message.
2 Think about the people and answer the questions:
- Who is the writer?
- Who is the reader?

PREPARE

Decide how to start and finish your messages. Try to use different expressions for each one.

WRITE

Write your messages, including the two sentences you chose from exercise 7. Use the examples in exercise 1 to help you.

Hi Gustavo, …

CHECK

Answer the questions.
1 Are the messages clear?
2 Do you use *because* correctly?
3 Do you use the present simple?

9 **Exchange your messages with another pair. Write replies to the messages and then return them to the writers.**

10 **Peer review** **Look at all the messages with your partner. Answer the questions.**

1 Are the messages clear and easy to understand?
2 Does the writer use *because* correctly to give a reason?
3 Does the writer use the present simple?

Grammar

Present simple

Affirmative

We use the present simple for routines and facts.
*I **start** school at nine o'clock.*
After *he/she/it*, most verbs end in *-s*.
*She **gets up** at 7:30.*
For verbs that end in *-s*, *-o*, *-ch*, *-sh*, *-x*, add *-es*.
*He **watches** TV after school. She **does** her homework.*
For verbs that end in consonant + *-y*, omit the *-y* and add *-ies*.
*He **studies** in the morning.*
Some verbs are irregular (*have – has*).
*She **has** dinner with her father.*

Negative

With *I/you/we/they*, we use *don't* + infinitive.
*I **don't** live in a city.*
With *he/she/it*, we use *doesn't* + infinitive.
*She **doesn't** like video games.*

Questions

Yes/No questions and short answers

Form *Yes/No* questions with *Do/Does* + subject + infinitive?
***Do** you like ice cream?* ***Does** he play tennis?*
Form short answers with *Yes* + subject + *do/does* or *No* + subject + *don't/doesn't*.
Use the contracted form in negative short answers.
***Yes**, I **do**./**No**, I **don't**.* ***Yes**, she **does**./**No**, she **doesn't**.*

Wh- questions

Form *Wh-* questions with Question word + *do/does* + subject + infinitive?
***Where** do you live?* ***What** time does he go to bed?*

Subject and object pronouns

Subject pronouns: I, you, he, she, it, we, they
Object pronouns: me, you, him, her, it, us, them
*Can **you** help **us**?*

Vocabulary

32 The time

five/ten/twenty/twenty-five/quarter/half **past** (six)
five/ten/twenty/twenty-five/quarter **to** (ten)
five o'clock; midday; midnight

33 Daily routines

do homework, finish school, get up, go home, go to bed, go to school, have breakfast, have dinner, have lessons, have lunch, relax, start school

34 Free-time activities

chat on my phone, do sport, go out on my bike, go shopping, go swimming, go to the cinema, listen to music, meet friends, play basketball, play the guitar, play the piano, play video games, read, sleep, take photos, watch TV

4 Project

WDYT?
(What do you think?)

Why is it a good idea to organise your time?

TASK: Make a digital poster about a typical day.

Learning outcomes

1 I can describe a typical day.
2 I can ask for help and give suggestions.
3 I can use appropriate language from the unit.

Graphic organiser → Project planner p131

1 Watch a video of students describing the typical day of a singer. What activities do they mention?

STEP 1: THINK

2 Look at the Model project. What can you see?

- the name of a famous person
- their photo
- a physical description
- photos of their day
- a short text about each photo

3 What do you think? Is the information real or invented?

STEP 2: PLAN

4 Work in pairs. Choose a famous person (a singer, actor, sports person, etc.).

5 Make notes about their typical day. (Invent!)

1 What does the person do? (make a list of eight things)
2 What time does the person do each thing?

STEP 3: CREATE

6 Work in pairs. Read tips in the Super skills box and practise saying the Key phrases with a partner.

COMMUNICATION SUPER SKILLS

Asking for help and giving suggestions

Tips

Ask questions about your ideas.
Say the things you like.
Give alternative ideas.

Key phrases

What do you think of this?
Is this a good idea?
Do you agree?
I like … a lot.
I'm not sure about …
What about … ?

7 Read the *How to …* tips on p131. Choose eight photos for your story. Use the tips and Key phrases in the Super skills box.

8 Write one or two sentences for each photo.

Grammar and Vocabulary
→ Quick review p57

Model project

1 Taylor Swift gets up at seven o'clock.

2 She has breakfast at quarter to eight. She usually has tea and toast.

3 At quarter past eight, she goes to the gym and she stays there for an hour.

4 In the morning, she goes shopping in New York City.

5 She has lunch with friends in a restaurant at half past one.

6 She doesn't relax in the afternoon. She practises singing or writes songs.

7 At eight o'clock, she sings in a concert. Then she meets her fans.

8 She goes to bed at midnight.

STEP 4: PRESENT

9 **Peer review** **Work with another pair. Take turns to describe your person's typical day. As you listen, answer the questions.**

1 Is the day organised? Is there a balance of activities?
2 Are the photos interesting?

4 FINAL REFLECTION

1 The task

Can you talk about times and activities in a typical day?

Do you use interesting photos?

2 Super skill

Do you ask for help and give suggestions?

3 Language

Do you use language from the unit? Give examples.

5 Tech life

WDYT?
(What do you think?)

Does technology make the world better? How?

Vocabulary: abilities; technology nouns; adjectives

Grammar: *can* and *can't*; *can*: questions and short answers; comparative adjectives; possessive pronouns

Reading: a web page about amazing robots

Listening: a talk about technology

Speaking: giving instructions

Writing: an advert

Project: design a robot to solve a problem

Video skills p61

Real-world speaking p67

Project pp70–71

Abilities

1 **Think of a video game you know where you do each of the actions in the box.**

call a friend cook dance ~~play (a musical instrument)~~ play (football, etc.) run sing walk

Play a musical instrument: Guitar Hero

2 **Complete the questions with some of the verbs in exercise 1.**

1. Which people in your family (…) dinner?
2. Do you (…) the piano, the guitar or another musical instrument?
3. Do you (…) songs in the shower?
4. How fast can you (…) 100 metres?
5. Which do you prefer to (…) : tennis or hockey?
6. Do you usually (…) your friends or text them?

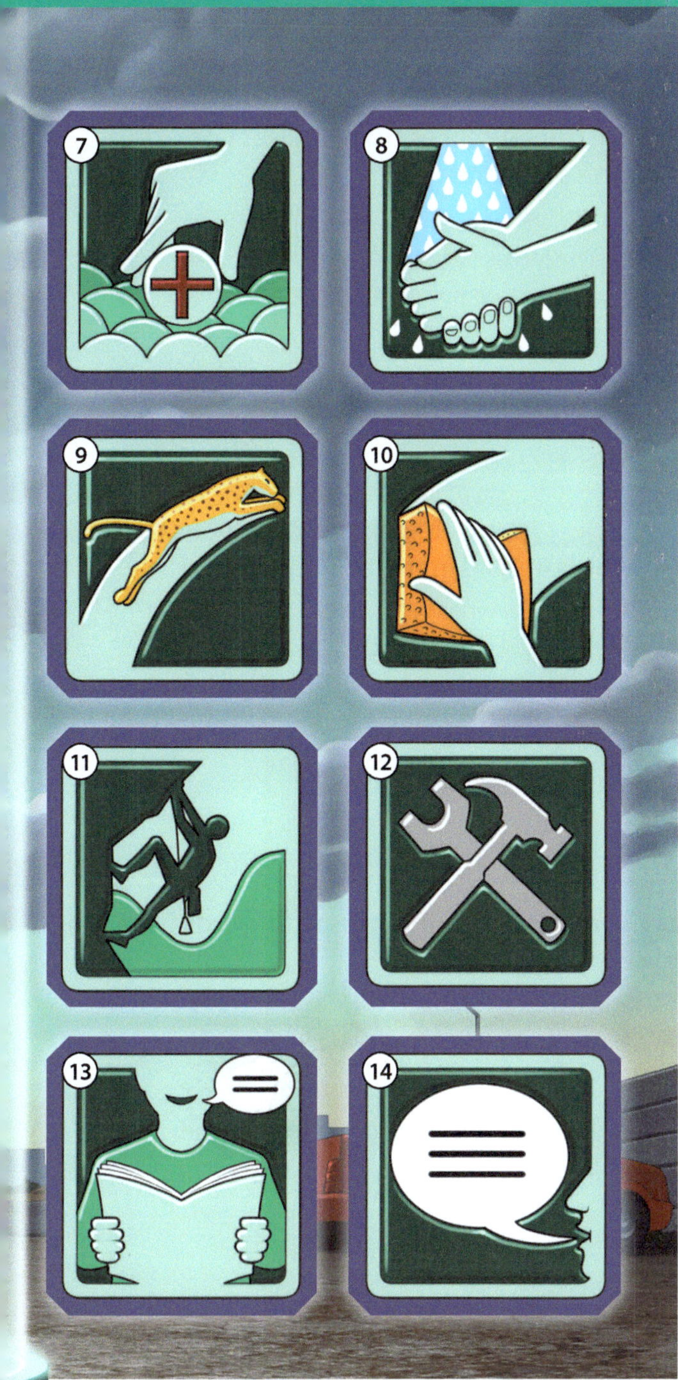

3 Look at the symbols from a video game. What abilities has the character got? Match abilities 1–14 with the words in the box.

add carry catch clean climb fly jump repair send speak spell talk tell stories wash

4 Choose the correct option.

1 **talk/jump** to your friend
2 **clean/speak** a language
3 **repair/wash** your face
4 **climb/jump** a mountain
5 **spell/tell stories** to your little cousin
6 **add/carry** numbers
7 **fly/send** a plane
8 **add/repair** a bike
9 **carry/jump** into a swimming pool

5 35 Add the missing verbs in the quiz and choose the correct option. Then listen and check.

1 If you (...) all the numbers from 1 to 100, the answer is **500/5,050/55,000**.

2 People (...) the word 'colour' C-O-L-O-R in **the UK/Australia/the USA**.

3 World record holder, Ronald Sarchian can (...) **52/72/92** tennis balls in one minute.

4 A typical American (...) and receives **34/64/94** text messages every day.

5 Ebin George from India can (...) **17/27/37** musical instruments, including the violin, piano and guitar.

6 Ziad Fazah from Liberia can (...) **19/39/59** languages!

7 **A kangaroo/A dolphin/A flea** can (...) 200 times its body length.

8 It takes about three **weeks/months/years** to (...) all of the Burj Khalifa's 24,000 windows.

VIDEO SKILLS

6 Watch the video. What does the narrator make?

7 Work in pairs. Answer the questions.

1 Why do people watch 'how to' videos like this?
2 Why do we only see the vlogger's hands in this video?
3 Videos are a great way to learn how to make things.' Do you agree or disagree?

A web page

1 Work in pairs. Write all the ability verbs and phrases you can remember. You have one minute!

add numbers, …

2 Work in pairs. What are the similarities and differences between the photos?

A

B

3 Look at the photos of robots in the article. Which of the abilities in exercise 1 do you think each robot has got?

I think robot A runs.

Really? I don't. But I think it walks.

4 Read the web page quickly. Check your answers in exercise 3.

Subskill: Reading for specific information

Before you read again, write words you think are in the text to help you find information, e.g. car, kitchen, piano, parts.

5 36 Read and listen to the web page. Copy and complete the table with the names and abilities of the robots in the article.

Robot	Abilities

6 Are the sentences true or false? Correct the false sentences.

1 Walker can move in different ways.
2 The Moley Robotic Kitchen has got a complete body.
3 The Moley Robotic Kitchen only cooks meals.
4 Lindsey works in a café.
5 Most robots are cheap.
6 Nybble costs less than other robots.

7 **Word work** Match the definitions to the words in bold in the text.

1 a person who helps visitors and gives information
2 an adjective that means you want to eat
3 an animal that lives in your home as part of your family
4 people who buy things in shops
5 have a particular price
6 you use these to walk up and down in a building

8 Complete the sentences with words from exercise 7.

1 We haven't got a (…) ; Mum doesn't like animals.
2 **A:** How can I go up to the clothes department?
B: The (…) are over there.
3 I'm very (…) . Why don't we get a sandwich?
4 This bike (…) €800 – it's very expensive.
5 There aren't any (…) in the shops today.
6 I'd like to visit the old part of town. Why don't we go with a (…) ?

CRITICAL THINKING SUPER SKILLS

1 **Remember** Which of the robots in the text do you think are useful?

2 **Analyse** Which of these things are advantages of robots? Which are disadvantages?

a Robots cost a lot of money.
b Robots learn quickly.
c Robots don't get tired.
d Robots can do dangerous or boring jobs.
e Robots can become more intelligent than people.
f Robots can't do a lot of things that people can do.

3 **Evaluate** What do you think: is it a good idea to have robots? Why?

Amazing ROBOTS!

There are many different types of robots today – here are four of our favourites.

Our first robot is Walker. What can Walker do? Well, he can walk, of course, but Walker can also dance, climb **stairs** and prepare drinks. He's also got some cool musical abilities: he can't sing, but he can play the piano!

It's dinner time and you're feeling **hungry**. You'd like to eat your favourite spaghetti dish, but you don't want to cook today. What can you do? You can use the Moley Robotic Kitchen. These robot arms can prepare your favourite meal and then clean the kitchen while you eat!

And this is not the only working robot. Visit Lincoln Museum in England and you can meet a robot **guide**: Lindsey. She answers visitors' questions and gives information about the things in the museum. And there's a café in Istanbul where robot waiters serve the **customers**!

If your parents don't want an animal in the house, why not ask them for a robot **pet**? Most robots **cost** thousands of dollars, but can you have a robot pet for less money? Yes, you can. Nybble is a robot cat and it can walk, run and climb. But the most important thing is that you can make Nybble yourself and it only costs $200.

A

B

C

D

can and *can't*

1 Copy and complete the tables with the examples in the box.

> You can meet a robot guide.
> Walker can't sing.

Affirmative/Negative		
Subject	***can***	**infinitive**
She 1 (...)	can 2 (...)	play the guitar. 3 (...)
Subject	***can't* (*cannot*)**	**infinitive**
They 4 (...)	can't 5 (...)	swim. 6 (...)

2 Choose the correct option to complete the rules.

1 After *can*, we **use/don't use** another verb.
2 We use the infinitive **with/without** *to* after *can*.
3 After *he/she/it*, *can* **ends/doesn't end** in *-s*.
4 We form the negative with ***don't can/can't*** + infinitive.

3 Write affirmative and negative sentences with the information in the table.

	speak French	**drive a car**	**cook a meal**
I	(+)	(-)	(-)
You	(-)	(-)	(+)
Joel	(-)	(+)	(-)
Lisa and Harry	(+)	(-)	(-)

I can speak French.

4 Complete the text with *can/can't* and the verbs in brackets.

In the robot band Z-Machines, Ashura plays the drums. He **1** (...) **(talk -)** to his fans, but he **2** (...) **(play +)** very well because he's got 22 arms! The guitarist, Mach, **3** (...) **(sing +)** and he **4** (...) **(make +)** the same sound as eight human musicians because he's got 78 fingers! The robots **5** (...) **(write -)** music, but they **6** (...) **(play +)** and never get tired!

can: questions and short answers

5 Read the examples and add them to the table.

> What can Walker do?
> Can you have a robot pet? Yes, you can.

***Yes/No* questions**			
Can	**subject**	**infinitive?**	
Can 1 (...)	he 2 (...)	fly a plane? 3 (...)	
Yes/No,	**subject**	***can/can't***	
No, 4 (...)	he 5 (...)	can't. 6 (...)	
***Wh-* questions**			
Question word	***can***	**subject**	**infinitive?**
What sport 7 (...)	can 8 (...)	you 9 (...)	play? 10 (...)

6 Write complete questions.

1 play a musical instrument ?
What instrument / play ?
Can you play a musical instrument?
What instrument can you play?
2 run 100 metres ?
How fast / run / it ?
3 cook ?
What type of food / cook ?
4 your best friend / speak another language ?
Which language / speak ?
5 your mum or dad / play a video game well ?
Which game / play ?

7 Work in pairs. Ask and answer the questions in exercise 6.

8 Answer the question to solve the Brain teaser.

Reinforcement and Challenge → Grammar bootcamp p122

Technology nouns; adjectives

1 Match objects A–H in the photos with the words in the box.

camera charger keyboard laptop
screen speaker tablet touchpad

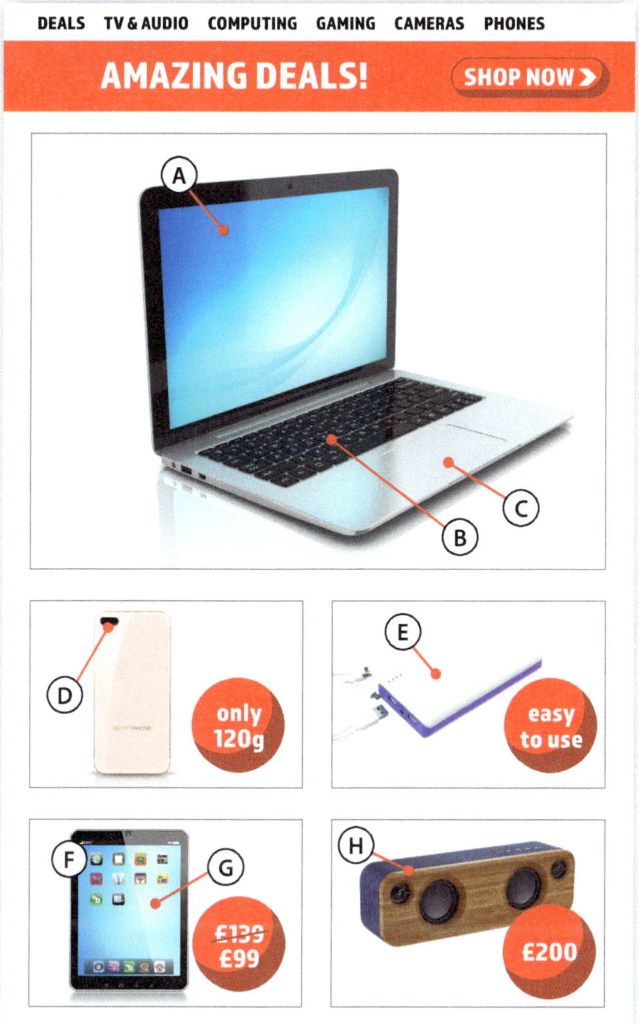

2 Work in pairs. Which of the objects do you use?

I use my brother's laptop.

I use a laptop, but I never use a tablet.

3 Match adjectives 1–4 with their opposites a–d.

1 cheap   **a** slow
2 difficult   **b** light
3 fast   **c** expensive
4 heavy   **d** easy

4 Describe the objects in exercise 1 using the adjectives in exercise 3.

The laptop is fast.

A talk

5 Look at photos 1–3. What are the objects? What do you think they can do?

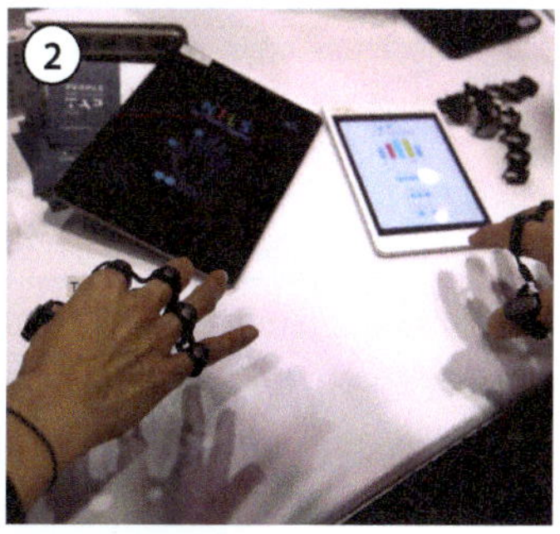

6 37 Listen to a talk about technology. The speaker talks about the objects in exercise 5. Write the order that he talks about them.

Subskill: Completing a table

Sometimes you need to choose more than one answer. Keep listening to all the information.

7 Copy and complete the table. Listen again and choose all the things that you can do with each object.

You can ...	watch	camera	keyboard
wear it	✓		
talk to friends			
watch films			
walk and write messages			
take photos			
use the internet			
make videos			

8 Work in pairs. Which object in exercise 5 would you like to have? Choose one and say why.

I'd like the keyboard. I write a lot of messages.

Really? I'd like the ...

Pronunciation: Spelling the sound /iː/ → p129

Vocabulary extension → Workbook p104

Comparative adjectives

1 Read the examples. Choose the correct option to complete the rules.

> This camera is smaller than a golf ball.
> This is better than a phone. The screen is bigger.
> An old camera is heavier than a new camera.
> New technology isn't more expensive.

1 We use comparative adjectives to compare **two/three or more** things.
2 After comparative adjectives, we use ***that/than***.

2 Write the comparative adjectives and adjectives in exercise 1.

smaller – small

3 Match rules a–e with the comparative adjectives in exercise 2.

a two-syllable adjectives ending in *-y* → ~~*-y*~~ + *-ier*
b one-syllable adjectives → + *-er*
c adjectives with two or more syllables → *more* + adjective
d some adjectives have an irregular comparative form
bad – worse
e one-syllable adjectives ending in one vowel + one consonant (but not ending in *-w* or *-y*) → double the final consonant + *-er*

4 Write the comparative form of the adjectives in the box.

> ~~beautiful~~ cheap difficult easy fast light new old slow thin

beautiful – more beautiful

5 Write sentences to compare the laptop and the tablet.

1	2.5 kilos	1 kilo
2	15″	9.5″
3	easy to use **	easy to use ****
4	€350	€240
5	good	excellent

1 The laptop is heavier than the tablet.

Possessive pronouns

6 Read the examples. Match subject pronouns 1–6 with the possessive pronouns.

> I use mine to talk to friends. (= my phone)
> Their camera is better than ours. (= our camera)
> My screen is smaller than yours. (= your screen)

Possessive pronouns
hers his mine ours theirs yours

1 I 2 you 3 he 4 she 5 we 6 they

1 I – mine

7 Complete the sentences with possessive pronouns.

1 Is this your tablet? It isn't (…) . Maria's got a tablet like that. Perhaps it's (…) .
2 That's Toni and Ben's computer. And the charger is (…) , too.
3 I haven't got a laptop, but my dad's got one. I often use (…) .
4 I really like your phone. My phone is old, but (…) is new.

8 Choose the correct option.

GRAMMAR ROUND-UP

1 2 3 4 5 **6 7 8**

Madhav Lavakare **1 is/are** a teenager from India. He **2 go/goes** to school every day, and he also invents things using technology. He **3 's/'ve** got some great ideas!

These glasses are one of them. They're for people who can't hear! There **4 's/are** a small computer on the glasses. When a person speaks, the words appear on a screen in front of the glasses, and the deaf person can **5 read/to read** them.

Madhav makes **6 theirs/his** glasses with a 3D printer, so they're **7 more cheap/cheaper** than similar technology. This means that **8 any/a lot of** deaf people in India can buy them.

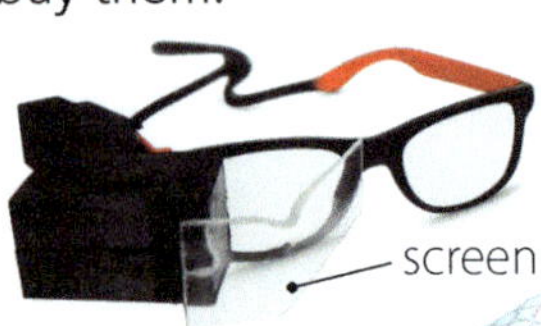

Reinforcement and Challenge → Grammar bootcamp p123

Giving instructions

1 **Work in pairs. What can you do? Is it easy or difficult?**

1 make a website
2 use a 3D printer
3 share photos on social media
4 download an app

2 **Match instructions 1–4 with pictures A–D.**

1 Click on 'save'.
2 Press 'print'.
3 Go to a website.
4 Open a file.

A

B

C
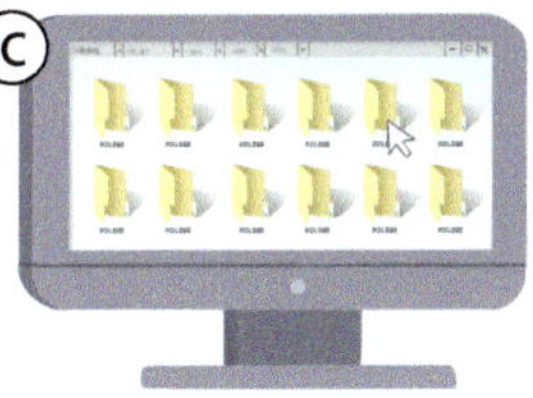

D

3 **Watch the video. What are the instructions for?**

4 **Watch again. Which Key phrases do you hear?**

5 **Complete the dialogue with the Key phrases. Watch again and check.**

Kelly: Hey, guess what! My dad has a new 3D printer.

Connor: Really?

Kelly: Yes, it's better than a normal printer. You can make objects with it.

Connor: Wow! **1** (…) do you do that?

Kelly: Well, **2** (…) go to a website and choose a model. Then click on 'save'.

Connor: **3** (…) next?

Kelly: **4** (…) you open the file on your computer, and select the printer.

Connor: Right.

Kelly: And **5** (…), send the instructions to the printer, and click print!

Connor: Can you **6** (…)?

Kelly: Sure. Come on.

6 **Create your own dialogue. Follow the steps in the Skills boost.**

SKILLS BOOST

THINK
Choose instructions to write. Choose one of the options in exercise 1 or use your own idea.

PREPARE
Prepare a dialogue. Include Key phrases for asking for and giving instructions.
How do you … ?

PRACTISE
Practise your dialogue. Take turns to ask for and give instructions.

PERFORM
Act out your dialogue for the class.

7 **Peer review** **Listen to your classmates and answer the questions.**

1 Are the instructions clear?
2 How many Key phrases do they use?

Key phrases

Asking for instructions:

How do you … (make an object on a 3D printer/make a website/share photos …)?
What's next?
Can you show me?

Giving instructions:

First, (go to) …
Then, (click on) …
Next, (open) …
(And) finally, (click) …

US → UK

My dad has a new 3D printer. (US) → My dad's got a new 3D printer. (UK)
Click print! (US) → Press print! (UK)

Technology ▾ | Price ▾ | Condition ▾ | Location ▾

Laptop for sale!

This laptop is perfect for students! You can use it to do homework and play games. It's smaller and lighter than other laptops. The touchpad and the keyboard are easy to use. It's a beautiful blue colour, and it comes with a free charger.

It's only two years old and it's in excellent condition.
You can buy it now for only €75. It's a bargain!

Friday 24th February 97 4

Portable speaker

Are you a music fan? Then this speaker is for you. It's small, but the sound quality is better than you get from a bigger speaker. You can connect it to your computer, tablet or phone. It's lighter than other speakers, so you can carry it from room to room. It's only six months old, and it comes with a book of instructions.

Colour: black
Price: €40

Wednesday 9th March 130 5

Portable charger

Sony PlayStation 4 games console

An advert

1 **Work in pairs. Answer the questions.**

1 What are the objects in the photos?
2 What type of website is this?

2 **Read the adverts. Would you like to buy one of these things? Why/Why not?**

3 **Read the adverts again. Answer the questions for the laptop and the speaker.**

1 Who is the object good for?
2 What are the good things about it?
3 What colour is it?
4 How old is it?
5 What is the price?

▶ Subskill: Spelling

It's important to use correct spelling when you write. Think about:

- silent letters, e.g. cam(e)ra
- double letters, e.g. thinner
- pronunciation and spelling, e.g. cheap /iː/, screen /iː/

4 38 **Close your books. Listen and write the words you hear.**

5 **Work in pairs. Compare your spelling in exercise 4.**

6 **Find the words in the adverts and check their spelling.**

Writing competence → Workbook pp116–117

7 **Correct one spelling mistake in each sentence.**

1 This phone isn't dificult to use.
2 The speakers are forteen years old.
3 You can write to me at this adress.
4 This laptop is heavyer than other laptops.
5 You can take fotos with this phone.

8 **Write an advert for an object you want to sell. Follow the steps in the Skills boost.**

SKILLS BOOST

THINK

Choose an object to sell. You can use one of the objects in exercise 1 or another object, e.g. a mobile phone, a tablet, a bike, a bag.

PREPARE

1 Make notes about the object. Answer the questions in exercise 3.
It's a phone.
It's good for students, for …
2 Look at the advert in exercise 2. Find phrases that you can use in your advert.
… for sale!
It's in excellent condition.

WRITE

Write your advert. Remember to use:

- *can/can't*
- adjectives to describe the object
- comparatives

CHECK

Read your advert. Answer the questions.

1 Do you say what you can do with this object?
2 Do you compare the object to other similar objects?
3 Is your spelling correct?

9 **Peer review** **Work in groups. Read your classmates' adverts and answer the questions.**

1 Which object do you want to buy? Why?
2 Is the spelling correct in the advert?

QUICK REVIEW 5

Grammar

can and *can't*

We use *can/can't* to talk about ability.
After *can/can't*, we use the infinitive of the verb without *to*. There's no *-s* with *he/she/it*.

Questions and short answers

To make a question, use: (Question word) + *can* + subject + infinitive.
__Can you__ draw? Yes, I __can__./No, I __can't__.
What __can__ you do?

Comparative adjectives

We use comparative adjectives to compare two things.
After comparative adjectives, we use *than*.
This phone is __smaller than__ that phone.
This printer is __more expensive than__ other printers.
To make a comparative adjective:
For one-syllable adjectives, add *-er* *small__er__, light__er__*
For most one-syllable adjectives ending in consonant + vowel + consonant (not ending in *-w*), double the final consonant and add *-er* *bi__gger__, ho__tter__, thi__nner__*
For two-syllable adjectives ending in *-y*, omit the *y* and add *-ier* *heav__ier__, easier*
For adjectives with two or more syllables, use *more* + adjective *__more__ expensive, __more__ difficult*
Some adjectives have irregular comparative forms
good → __better__, bad → __worse__

Possessive pronouns

We use a possessive pronoun to talk about possession when there is no noun after it.
Is this David's phone? *No, it's __mine__.*
Is that Katy's laptop? *Yes, it's __hers__.*

Subject pronoun	I	you	he	she	we	they
Possessive pronoun	mine	yours	his	hers	ours	theirs

Vocabulary

39 Abilities

add, call a friend, carry, catch, clean, climb, cook, dance, fly, jump, play (a musical instrument), play (football), repair, run, send, sing, speak, spell, talk, tell stories, walk, wash

40 Technology nouns

camera, charger, keyboard, laptop, screen, speaker, tablet, touchpad

41 Adjectives

cheap, difficult, easy, expensive, fast, heavy, light, slow

5 Project

WDYT? (What do you think?)

Does technology make the world better? How?

TASK: Design a robot to solve a problem.

Learning outcomes

1 I can design a robot and explain the problem that it solves.

2 I can find new solutions to problems.

3 I can use appropriate language from the unit.

Graphic organiser → Project planner p132

1 Watch a video of students practising their robot presentation. What problem does the robot solve?

STEP 1: THINK

2 Complete the notes. Write the phrases in the box in the correct place.

in her kitchen   David's grandmother, Elena
she's short and can't get things from high places
when she wants to cook a meal

THE PROBLEM

Who? **1** (...)   Where? **3** (...)
What? **2** (...)   When? **4** (...)

3 How does Long Arm Luke solve the problem? Match 1–4 with a–d.

1 Elena can give
2 It's small and moves
3 It's plastic and it's lighter
4 It's easier for Elena to get things and

a than other robots.
b instructions and the robot helps.
c she's more independent.
d on wheels.

STEP 2: PLAN

4 Work in groups of three. Think of a problem and make notes. Use the questions in exercise 2 to help you.

5 Read the tips in the Super skills box and practise saying the Key phrases with your group.

CREATIVITY SUPER SKILLS

Finding new solutions to problems

Tips

Work together and listen to everyone's ideas.

Use your imagination.

Remember – your ideas need to solve the problem!

Key phrases

What do you think?	*Don't forget ...*
Let's listen to (Jon).	*That's a good idea.*
Why don't we (+ verb)?	*That's great!*

6 Work together to design a robot that can solve your problem. Use the tips and Key phrases in the Super skills box.

STEP 3: CREATE

7 Read the *How to ...* tips on p132 and prepare your presentation.

- Slide 1: Explain the problem.
- Slide 2: Introduce your robot.
- Slide 3: Give more information, e.g. a description of the robot's abilities, comparing the robot with other solutions.
- Slide 4: Say how it solves the problem.

Grammar and Vocabulary → Quick review p69

Model project

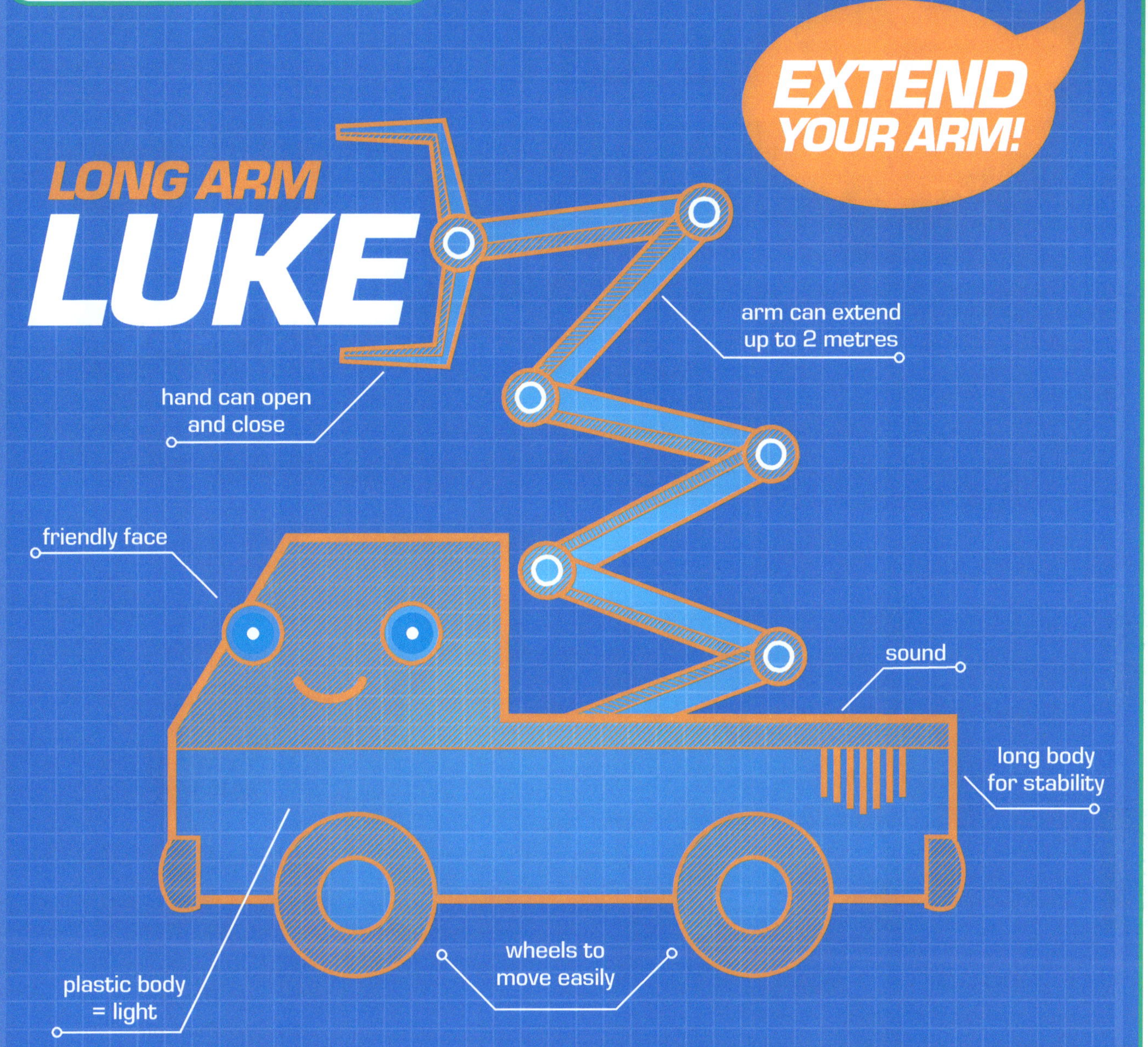

STEP 4: PRESENT

8 Peer review **Give your digital presentation and listen to other groups' presentations. As you listen, answer the questions.**

1. Do you think the robot is a good solution to the problem?
2. Ask a question about the robot.
3. What differences are there between your robots?

5 FINAL REFLECTION

1. **The task**
   Is the digital presentation clear and attractive?
   Can you explain your robot clearly?
2. **Super skill**
   Do you find new solutions to the problem? Give examples.
3. **Language**
   In your presentation, do you use language from the unit? Give examples.

6 The world is art

WDYT?
(What do you think?)

What is art?

Vocabulary: rooms and furniture; prepositions; clothes and accessories

Grammar: present continuous (affirmative, negative, questions and short answers)

Reading: an entertainment guide about escape rooms

Listening: a radio programme from an art workshop

Speaking: asking for information

Writing: text messages

Project: make a video guide for a photo exhibition

Video skills p73

Real-world speaking p79

Project pp82–83

WELCOME TO THE UPSIDE-DOWN HOUSE!

Do you like new experiences? Then visit the UK's first upside-down house. All the furniture is on the ceiling and not on the floor!

It's crazy and it's fun – and it's a great place to take photos!

Rooms and furniture; prepositions

1 **Look at the photos and read about the house. Answer the questions.**

1. What's different about the house?
2. Is there a house like this in your country?
3. Would you like to visit it? Why/Why not?

2 **Match photos A–E with the words in the box. There are two extra words.**

bathroom	bedroom	dining room	garden	hall	kitchen	living room

3 **Where do people usually do these things? Write the room or place in a house.**

1. cook
2. sleep
3. watch TV with other people
4. wash their face and hands
5. have dinner
6. play ball games

6 Read the sentences about the photos. Write a preposition for diagrams a–i.

1 There's a bed **in** the bedroom.
2 **Near** the bed, there's a small table with a clock **on** it.
3 The woman is **above** the table!
4 In the living room, the chair is **between** the table and the wall.

a (...)	b *in*	c (...)	d (...)	e (...)

5 In the bathroom, the toilet is **under** the woman.
6 There's a window **behind** the woman.
7 There's a 'welcome' mat **in front of** the door in the hall.
8 There are some shoes **next to** the 'welcome' mat.

f (...)	g (...)	h (...)	i (...)

7 Choose the correct option to describe the photos.

1 The woman is **under/above** the chair in the living room.
2 She's **in/on** a cupboard in the kitchen.
3 The window in the kitchen is **between/behind** two cupboards.
4 In the hall, the door is **in front of/behind** the woman.
5 There are some jackets **next to/between** the door.

4 Work in pairs. Draw a plan of your house or flat. Then show your plan to your partner and describe it.

This is my flat. It's got three bedrooms. This is the door and this is ...

5 Answer the questions about the words in the box.

bath bed chair ceiling floor shower table toilet wall

1 Which three things are in all the photos?
2 Which two things are not in the photos?
3 In which photos can you see the other four things?

VIDEO SKILLS

8 Watch the video. What rooms do you see?

9 Work in pairs. Answer the questions.

1 Why do you think Theo and Bee made the documentary?
2 Why do they use music in the video?

Pronunciation: /e/ and /ɜː/ → p129

Vocabulary extension → Workbook p105

An entertainment guide

1 **Read the description of a room and draw the picture. Then show your picture to your classmates. Are the pictures the same?**

This is a picture of a bedroom. There's a bed between the door and a desk. There's a laptop on the desk and a chair in front of it. There's a window above the desk. Next to the window, above the bed, there's a big picture of a beach. There's a ball under the bed. There's a school bag near the door with a guitar behind it.

2 **Work in pairs. Look at rooms A–C in the entertainment guide. What kind of rooms and furniture can you see?**

3 **Look at the entertainment guide and read the description of an escape room in the box. Why do we call it an escape room?**

4 42 **Read and listen to the text. Match photos A–C with texts 1–3.**

5 **In which room do players … ?**

1 start in a different country
2 go to more than one room
3 help a famous doctor
4 meet something dangerous
5 go to someone's home
6 travel to another time

Subskill: Answering true or false questions

Read each sentence first. Look for a reason to decide if a sentence is true or false.

6 **Read the text again. Are the sentences true or false? Give reasons for your answers.**

1 Escape rooms are open on Saturdays and Sundays.
2 You meet a person from the Wizarding School.
3 There are people in the museum in Room 33.
4 The Sherlock game starts in his living room.
5 You've always got one hour to escape from an escape room.
6 There are dangerous situations in some games.

7 **Word work** **Match the definitions to the words in bold in the text.**

1 an adjective to describe something that you can't find
2 we put flowers in this
3 objects or facts that help you to solve a puzzle
4 this person is similar to a king, but more important
5 an imaginary, not real, living thing that is scary
6 an action or activity that isn't legal

8 **Complete the sentences with words from exercise 7.**

1 You call the police when you see a (…) .
2 A lot of people go to Scotland to see the Loch Ness (…) .
3 Japan is the only country in the world today with an (…) .
4 Our school keeps all (…) objects in a special room.
5 We've got a blue (…) on the table in our dining room.
6 I can't do this puzzle. The (…) are really difficult!

CRITICAL THINKING

SUPER SKILLS

1 **Remember** Read the text again. What do people do to escape from each room?

2 **Analyse** Why do you think escape rooms are so popular? Think about:
- real-life games
- fantasy – you're a different person
- the people you play with
- it's a different world
- the time limit
- you solve puzzles

3 **Create** Imagine you want to create an escape room. Think of a situation or story for your room. Think about these questions:
1 Where are the players?
2 When is the story happening?
3 What is the problem?
4 What do the players do to escape?
5 Are there any surprises in the room? (e.g. a monster!)

Research

Find out if there is an escape room where you live. What is the situation or story?

An **ESCAPE ROOM** is a real-life adventure game. Players find **clues** and solve puzzles to escape from the room. The clues can be anywhere: under a table, behind a picture or on the ceiling! You need to find them!

THE GREAT ESCAPE!

If you're looking for something different to do this weekend, why not try one of London's top escape rooms?

A

1 SHERLOCK: THE GAME IS NOW

Sherlock Holmes is travelling in another country, and Dr Watson needs your help. The game starts in a shop, and Watson gives you instructions in a video. A few minutes later, you're standing in the living room of 221b Baker Street. There are books on the floor and papers on the walls. Can you find the **clues** and solve the **crime**? Be careful, someone is watching you!

Time: 100 minutes

3–6 players

B

2 THE WIZARDING SCHOOL

You're a student of magic and you're looking for a **lost** object. A teacher at the Wizarding School takes you to the first room. There are pictures on the walls and an old book on the desk. You need to solve the puzzle to go to the next room. In the final room, you find the object, but … a **monster** is waiting for you. Can you solve the puzzle to kill the monster?

Time: 60 minutes

3–6 players

C

3 ROOM 33

In this game, you're a time-traveller. You aren't living in the 21st century. You're working for the Chinese **Emperor** in 1675. One night, a special **vase** disappears, and you need to find it. The problem is that the vase is now in the British Museum. You travel in time to the present day. The museum is empty, but there are lasers in front of the vase. Can you get it?

Time: 60 minutes

3–6 players

fun facts

The idea of escape rooms comes from Japan. Now escape rooms are very popular in Europe. Athens, in Greece, has got a three-hour escape room experience!

The longer read → Resource centre

Present continuous: affirmative and negative

1 Read the examples. Copy and complete the table.

Sherlock Holmes is travelling in another country.
He isn't watching you.
I'm standing in the living room of 221b Baker Street.
You aren't living in the 21st century.

Affirmative		
I	**1** (…)	standing in the living room. travelling in another country.
You/We/They	're	
He/She/It	**2** (…)	
Negative		
I	'm not	watching you. living in the 21st century.
You/We/They	**3** (…)	
He/She/It	**4** (…)	

2 Answer the questions.

1 What do we use before verb *-ing* to make the present continuous?
2 Do we use the present continuous to talk about habits, or things happening now?

3 Write the *-ing* form of the verbs. Then match a–c with rules 1–3.

a	b	c
speak – *speaking*	have – *having*	sit – *sitting*
go	make	chat
walk	ride	run
play	dance	shop
read	write	swim

1 Verbs that end in *-e*, omit *-e* and add *-ing*.
2 Most verbs that end in a consonant + vowel + consonant, double the final consonant and add *-ing*.
3 For most verbs, add *-ing*.

4 Complete the sentences with the present continuous form of the verbs in brackets.

1 We (…) **(do)** an English exercise at the moment.
2 I (…) **(write)** in my notebook.
3 The teacher (…) **(talk)** to the class.
4 My friend (…) **(sit)** next to me.
5 We (…) **(speak)** in English.

Time expressions

We often use time expressions with the present continuous: *today*, *now*, *at the moment*.

5 Write the sentences in the present continuous.

1 I / not chat / on my phone now
I / read
I'm not chatting on my phone now. I'm reading.
2 Evan / not do / his homework
He / play / a video game
3 My friends / not listen / to music
They / sing
4 I / not ride / my bike today
I / walk / to school
5 We / not watch / TV at the moment
We / have / dinner

6 Complete the email with the present continuous form of the verbs in brackets.

To: Jodie Monday

Hi Jodie,

I **1** (…) **(write)** to tell you about my art project at school. We **2** (…) **(learn)** about different artists, and I **3** (…) **(do)** a project about Elisabeth Anisimow. She's a teenager from Los Angeles. She doesn't paint pictures. She paints people and then she takes a photo of them.

In this picture, a boy **4** (…) **(sit)** on a small chair, and a girl **5** (…) **(give)** him some milk. They **6** (…) **(not wear)** old clothes. Elisabeth paints the clothes so that they look old. And the girl **7** (…) **(not hold)** an old bottle. Elisabeth paints all the furniture and objects too!

I **8** (…) **(not send)** the other pictures because you can find them online. I hope you like them!

Ed

7 Answer the question to solve the Brain teaser.

BRAIN TEASER

Five brothers are sitting in the living room. Joel is reading a book, Will is playing chess, Tom is writing an email, and Alan is doing his homework.

What is the other brother doing?

Clothes and accessories

1 **Match clothes 1–9 with the words in the box.**

coat dress jacket jeans shirt shoes skirt trainers trousers

2 **Complete the sentences with the words in the box.**

glasses jacket trainers umbrella

1 You use an (…) if it's raining.
2 Most people wear (…) for sport.
3 Some people wear (…) to help them see.
4 You can wear a (…) on top of a shirt.

3 **Match 1–4 with a–d to make sentences.**

1 You **put on** your clothes
2 You **take off** your jacket
3 You **wear** trainers
4 You **carry** an umbrella

a to do sport.
b when it's raining.
c when you get up in the morning.
d when you arrive home.

4 **Complete the sentences with the verbs in bold in exercise 3.**

1 In Japan, people (…) their shoes when they go into a house.
2 I only (…) glasses for reading.
3 It's cold today. (…) your jacket before you leave.
4 Can you (…) this bag for me?

A radio programme

5 **Read the website from an art workshop.**

HOME ABOUT PROJECTS CONTACT COMMUNITY

Street Style Surgery works with children and teenagers in schools and clubs. Activities include music, graffiti art, dance and fashion.

A Modelling T-shirts in a fashion show

B Using spray paints

C Preparing designs

D The finished T-shirts

▶ Subskill: Using photo captions to help you understand

Notice the vocabulary in the captions. You will probably hear it when you listen.

6 🔊43 **Listen to a school radio programme. Put photos A–D in exercise 5 in the correct order.**

7 **Sentences 1–4 are false. Listen again and correct them.**

1 Cara is in Year 9.
2 All the students make their own designs.
3 The students don't like this activity.
4 The students are using spray paint to do graffiti.

8 **Work in pairs. Discuss the questions.**

1 Would you like to do this activity? Why/Why not?
2 Is there another activity in the information box about Street Style Surgery that you prefer?

Present continuous: *Yes/No* questions and short answers

1 Read the examples. Choose the correct option to complete the rules.

Are you having a good time? Yes, we are.
Are the teenagers making their own designs? No, they aren't.

1 In *Yes/No* questions, the verb *be* comes **before/ after** the subject.
2 We make the short answer **with the main verb/ with the verb *be***.
3 In short answers, we **use/don't use** contractions in the affirmative.
4 In short answers, we **use/don't use** contractions in the negative.

2 Write questions.

1 he / wear / a jacket ?
Is he wearing a jacket?
2 they / listen / music ?
3 we / travel / by bus ?
4 you / watch / a film ?
5 I / speak / Spanish ?
6 she / play / the guitar ?

3 Look at the photo. Write questions and short answers.

1 the girl in the orange T-shirt / wear /glasses ?
Is the girl in the orange T-shirt wearing glasses? No, she isn't.
2 the girl in the black T-shirt / wear / a watch ?
3 the girl on the right / hold / a phone ?
4 the girls / sit / in a classroom ?
5 the girl in the green and white T-shirt / wear / glasses ?
6 the girl in the middle / hold / a ball ?
7 two girls / wear / jeans ?

Present continuous: *Wh-* questions

4 Look at the examples in the table and order the words to make questions.

Question word	*be*	subject	verb *-ing*?
What	are	they	wearing?
Who	is	she	sitting with?

1 you / where / sitting / are ?
2 what language / you / are / speaking ?
3 you / what grammar / studying / are ?
4 teacher / wearing / your / is / what ?

5 Work in pairs. Ask and answer the questions in exercise 4.

6 Look at the photo. Then read the text and choose the correct option.

GRAMMAR ROUND-UP

1 2 3 4 5 6 7 8

A frog **1** (...) on someone's hand, ready to jump. Or is it? What **2** (...) looking at? Is it really a frog? **3** (...) . If you look carefully, **4** (...) that the frog is a painting! This is the work of an amazing artist, Iantha Naicker. Naicker **5** (...) and works in South Africa. She paints animals and other things on her hand. On her website you can see **6** (...) more examples of her work. **7** (...) tigers, pandas, fish and insects. Her paintings are amazing – I love **8** (...) !

	a	b	c
1	are sitting	is sitting	sit
2	are we	we are	do we
3	No, is not.	No, it isn't.	No, it is.
4	you do see	you can to see	you can see
5	living	lives	live
6	some	any	the
7	There are	There's	Have
8	it	him	them

Reinforcement and Challenge → Grammar bootcamp pp124–125

Asking for information

1 **What cartoons do you know? Would you like to visit a cartoon *museum*? Why/Why not?**

2 **Watch the video. Where is the museum? When is it open?**

3 **Watch again. Which two Key phrases do you not hear?**

4 **Complete the dialogue with the Key phrases. Watch again and check.**

Tourist officer: Good morning. Can **1** (…) ?

Leo: Hi. I'd like **2** (…) about this exhibition.

Tourist officer: OK, well, it's **3** (…) the Cartoon Museum.

Leo: Where's **4** (…) ?

Tourist officer: In Wells Street.

Leo: Wells Street?

Tourist officer: Near Oxford Circus station.

Leo: OK, great, we're staying near there. And what time **5** (…) ?

Tourist officer: It's open today **6** (…) .

Leo: How **7** (…) ?

Tourist officer: It's free if you're under 18.

Leo: Oh, great! Thank you.

Tourist officer: You're welcome. Goodbye.

1

2

5 **Create your own dialogue. Follow the steps in the Skills boost.**

SKILLS BOOST

THINK

Think of a place to visit, for example an exhibition or a visitors' centre at a famous stadium.

Make notes about the following:

- the place
- where it is
- opening times
- the price

PREPARE

Prepare a dialogue about the visit. Remember to include Key phrases for asking about and giving information.

Hello, can I help you?

I'd like some information about …

PRACTISE

Practise your dialogue.

PERFORM

Act out your dialogue for the class.

6 **Peer review** **Listen to your classmates and answer the questions.**

1 Which Key phrases do they use?

2 Would you like to visit this place? Why/Why not?

Key phrases

Asking for information:

I'd like some information about (…)

Where's that?

What time is it open?

How much does it cost?

How can I get there?

Giving information:

Can I help you?

It's on at (…)

It costs (…)

It's open from (…) to (…)

Real-world grammar

We're staying near there.

Text messages

1 **Read the messages that Danny sends his friends. Then answer questions 1–3.**

1 Where does Danny want to go?

Danny wants to go to a graffiti event.

2 What are Danny's friends doing?

3 Can his friends meet him today?

2 **When we send text messages, we write in a shorter way. Read the examples of text language. Write each one as a full sentence.**

Using letters as words

1 What R U doing? **2** C U later.

Missing words

3 Want to come and see the graffiti artists?

4 See you Thursday.

5 You doing anything now?

Subskill: *so*

We use *so* when we want to describe the result of an action or situation.

3 **Read the example. Then answer the question.**

Danny wants to see the graffiti artists so he's texting his friends.

Why is Danny texting his friends? Because …

4 **Read the text messages in exercise 1 again. Find three examples with *so*.**

5 **Rewrite the sentences with *so* in the correct position.**

1 Jan's dad is from Berlin he can speak German.

2 It's raining we can't go running now.

3 Today's a holiday we haven't got school.

4 I haven't got any money I can't go to the cinema.

Writing competence → Workbook pp118–119

6 **Complete the examples with your own ideas.**

1 It's sunny today so …
2 I don't have football training today so …
3 I've got an exam tomorrow so …
4 I can't swim so …
5 I don't like pizza so …

7 **Write a text message dialogue. Follow the steps in the Skills boost.**

SKILLS BOOST

THINK

Work in pairs. Compare your sentences in exercise 6 and choose your favourite.

PREPARE

Prepare a dialogue. Include the following stages:

- Say hello.
- Invite your friend to do something with you or talk about a plan.
- Agree or disagree with the idea; give a reason.
- Say goodbye.

WRITE

Write your text message dialogue, based on your favourite sentence. Write at least six lines. Use the examples in exercise 1 to help you.

CHECK

Read your text messages and answer the questions.

1 Do you use the present continuous?
2 Do you use *so*?
3 Do you use any examples of text language?

8 **Peer review** **Exchange your text messages with other students. Answer the questions.**

1 What's the conversation about?
2 Does the writer use the present continuous correctly?
3 Does the writer use *so*?

Grammar

Present continuous

Affirmative and negative

We use the present continuous to describe things happening now.

We use the verb *be* + verb *-ing* to make the present continuous.

***I'm making** a video.* *He **isn't watching** a film.*

Spelling of verb + *-ing*

1 Most verbs → + *-ing*

*watch – watch**ing*** *wear – wear**ing***

2 Verbs ending in *e* → *e* + *-ing*

*make – mak**ing*** *write – writ**ing***

3 Most verbs ending in consonant + vowel + consonant → double the final consonant + *-ing*

*sit – sit**ting*** *swim – swim**ming***

Yes/No questions and short answers

In *Yes/No* questions, the verb *be* comes before the subject.

We make the short answer with the verb *be*. We don't use contracted forms in affirmative short answers.

Is he taking** photographs?* ***Yes, he is.

Are you doing** your homework?* ***No, I'm not.

Wh- questions

In *Wh-* questions, the order is question word + *be* + subject + verb *-ing*.

*What **are** they **doing**?*

*Where **are** you **going**?*

Time expressions with the present continuous

We use expressions like *today, now, at the moment* with the present continuous to describe actions happening now.

*I'm doing my homework **now**.*

*He isn't wearing trainers **today**.*

*Are you using this computer **at the moment**?*

Vocabulary

44 Rooms and furniture

bath, bathroom, bed, bedroom, ceiling, chair, dining room, floor, garden, hall, kitchen, living room, shower, table, toilet, wall

45 Prepositions

above, behind, between, in, in front of, near, next to, on, under

46 Clothes and accessories

Nouns: bag, coat, dress, glasses, hat, jacket, jeans, shirt, shoes, skirt, trainers, trousers, umbrella

Verbs: carry, put on, take off, wear

6 Project

WDYT? (What do you think?)

What is art?

TASK: Make a video guide for a photo exhibition.

Learning outcomes

1. I can describe people, places and what people are doing in a photo.
2. I can speak clearly when describing photos.
3. I can use appropriate language from the unit.

Graphic organiser → Project planner p132

1 Watch a video of students talking about the photos in their exhibition. Which photo are the students describing?

STEP 1: THINK

2 Work in pairs. Look at the photos. Are they interesting? Why?

3 Read the description of one of the photos in the Model project. Which questions does it answer?

1. What can you see in the photo?
2. Where are the people?
3. What are they doing?
4. What are they wearing?
5. Who is taking the photo?
6. Why is he/she taking the photo?
7. Why do the writers like the photo?

STEP 2: PLAN

4 Work in pairs. Choose four photos to include in your exhibition. You can choose photos from the internet or your own photos. How are your photos interesting?

5 Make notes about the photos. Answer the questions in exercise 3.

STEP 3: CREATE

6 Work in pairs. Read the tips in the Super skills box and practise saying the Key phrases with a partner.

COMMUNICATION SUPER SKILLS

Communicating clearly

Tips

Speak slowly and pronounce words clearly.

Speak loudly.

Make pauses so people have time to look at the photo and understand what you're saying.

Key phrases

That's very fast.

You're very quiet.

Try again.

Try to speak more loudly.

That's better.

I can't understand what you're saying.

7 Work in pairs. Practise reading your audio guide. Use the tips and Key phrases in the Super skills box.

8 Read the *How to …* tips on p132 and record your audio guide.

STEP 4: PRESENT

9 Present your photos and play your audio guide for other students.

Grammar and Vocabulary → Quick review p81

Model project

1

2

3

4

This is a photo of a group of young people. They're in front of a red wall and there's a red litter bin next to them. Some of the people are standing, some of them are sitting, and three people are upside-down. They're wearing similar clothes – trousers, jackets and trainers. The clothes are all different colours – blue, green, red, yellow, grey and orange.

This photo is an art project for school. The photographer is one of their friends. We like this photo because we like the colours and because the position of the people is interesting.

10 **Peer review** **As you listen to your classmates, answer the questions.**

1. Do they include a description of the people, the place and what the people are doing?
2. Is the photo interesting or unusual? Why?
3. Is the guide clear? Give reasons for your answer.

6 FINAL REFLECTION

1 The task

Do you describe people, places and what people are doing?

2 Super skill

Is your audio guide clear for other people? Say why.

3 Language

In your description of the photos, do you use language from the unit? Give examples.

7 Famous lives

WDYT? (What do you think?)

What does it mean to be famous?

Vocabulary: jobs; dates; adjectives to describe feelings

Grammar: past simple of *be*; past simple of regular and irregular verbs: affirmative

Reading: an article about celebrities past and present

Listening: a news report about teens and social media

Speaking: talking about last weekend

Writing: a description of a fictional character

Project: make a comic about an unknown hero

Video skills p85

Real-world speaking p91

Project pp94–95

Jobs; dates

1 **What jobs do the people in the photos do? Match people A–E with five of the words in the box.**

actor artist astronaut cook doctor farmer inventor singer teacher waiter

2 **Answer the questions with words from exercise 1.**

Who works in … ?

1 a hospital **3** the country **5** a studio
2 a kitchen **4** a school **6** a restaurant

3 47 **Look at the table and notice the stress patterns (O = stressed syllable, o = unstressed syllable). Listen and repeat the months.**

O	Oo	oO	Ooo	oOo
March	April	July	January	September

4 🔊48 **Listen to the other months. Then copy and complete the table in exercise 3 with the months in the box.**

February	May	June	August
October	November	December	

5 💬 **Work in pairs. Student A, say a month. Student B, say the next two months.**

March

April, May

6 Write the numbers in box A in words and match them with the ordinal numbers in box B.

A 1 2 3 4 5 6 17 18 20 22 29 31

B eighteenth fifth first fourth second seventeenth sixth third thirty-first twentieth twenty-ninth twenty-second

1: one – first

Language note

We say the date like this:
27th May = the twenty-seventh of May.
The two letters we write after the number are the final two letters of the ordinal number.

fir**st** – 1st	seco**nd** – 2nd
thi**rd** – 3rd	four**th** – 4th

7 When's your birthday? Ask three people in the class and note their answers.

8 🔊49 **Listen and write the dates.**

9 Which events on the calendar in exercise 1 do the dates in exercise 8 refer to?

VIDEO SKILLS

10 🎥 **Watch the video. What date is the video about?**

11 💬 **Work in pairs. Answer the questions.**

1. How do videos like this help people understand history?
2. Why did the vlogger make this video?
3. Are the photos and graphics in this video funny or serious? Why?

An article

1 **Work in pairs. Which three things do you think are the most important for a celebrity?**

- being in magazines and on TV
- having a lot of fans on social media
- being rich
- being famous with people of all ages
- selling things with your name

2 **Work in pairs. Name a celebrity who …**

1 is very popular on social media
2 is an actor or singer
3 is a sports star
4 does difficult or dangerous things
5 is an animal

Subskill: Reading in different ways

We read things in different ways. Move your eyes quickly over the text to find specific words. When you find them, read closely and intensively to check.

3 **Read the article quickly. Which type of celebrities in exercise 2 does it include?**

4 50 **Read more slowly and listen. Write their names.**

5 **Match celebrities 1–6 with descriptions a–f.**

1 Simone Biles
2 Laika
3 Ernest Shackleton
4 Alex Honnold
5 Doug the Pug
6 Gladiators

a does dangerous things now
b sports heroes of the past
c a famous dog in the 1950s
d a sports hero today
e a popular traveller and writer in the past
f an Instagram celebrity now

6 **Are the sentences true or false? Give reasons for your answers.**

1 Some present-day celebrities are sports stars.
2 There were photos of the best gladiators.
3 Alex Honnold is a singer.
4 Shackleton was famous for his travels in the Arctic.
5 One animal celebrity has got more than three million fans.
6 Laika was a hero all her life.

7 **Word work** **Match the definitions to the words in bold in the text.**

1 one hundred years
2 make something full
3 a small piece of paper with a design or picture on it that you buy and put on an envelope before you post it
4 big areas where people play sports, with lots of seats for other people to watch
5 exciting or dangerous experiences
6 travels to distant places

8 **Complete the sentences with words from exercise 7.**

1 Marco Polo is famous for his (…) to Mongolia and China.
2 The Bernabéu and the Wanda Metropolitano are two big (…) in Madrid.
3 I always (…) a bottle with water before I play basketball.
4 The Model T car by Ford was the winner of the 'Car of the 20th (…)' competition.
5 I love reading about the hero's (…) in the *Rebel of the Sands* books.
6 The (…) for a letter from Britain to Rio costs £1.35.

CRITICAL THINKING

SUPER SKILLS

1 **Understand** Work in pairs.
Write a list of five people who are celebrities for different reasons. Why is each one popular?

2 **Analyse** Look at some consequences of being a celebrity. Are they advantages (A), disadvantages (D) or it depends (ID)?

- You can't have any secrets.
- You have fans.
- Newspapers and TV want to know all about your life.
- All your fans want to take selfies with you.
- You have priority in restaurants and airports.
- People want you to look perfect all the time.
- You don't know if people are your real friends.
- You can get rich.

3 **Evaluate** Some celebrities do good things. Here are some examples. Can you think of any more good things celebrities do?

- Give money to charities (e.g. WWF)
- Be a good example (e.g. show how people can look after the environment)

Today there are a lot of celebrities, from YouTubers with millions of fans to world-famous singers with concerts that fill football stadiums. But is celebrity a new idea in the 21st century?

No, it isn't! Today we look at ...

CELEBRITIES past and present

Some of the most important celebrities today are sports stars like Usain Bolt, Simone Biles or Naomi Osaka. But were sporting heroes also celebrities in the past?

Yes, they were. In Roman times, gladiators were the sporting heroes of the day. Some gladiators were very popular, with lots of fans. There wasn't Instagram in Roman times, but there were paintings of the best gladiators.

People who do difficult or dangerous things, like climber Alex Honnold, often become celebrities. Ernest Shackleton was famous for his **expeditions** in Antarctica and he was a big celebrity at the start of the 20th century. He was a great communicator and stories of his **adventures** were popular with readers all over the world.

Today's celebrities aren't all people. The internet is full of celebrity animals like Doug the Pug, a dog with millions of followers on Instagram. But there were also celebrity animals in the past. On 3rd November 1957, a Russian dog, Laika, was the first animal astronaut. Laika was very famous in Russia, and in many countries there was a **stamp** with her picture. But Laika wasn't always a celebrity. Before she was a national hero, Laika was a street dog in Moscow.

fun facts Today, people go to special schools to learn to sing, dance and play football. In Roman times, there were gladiator schools!

The longer read → Resource centre

Past simple of *be*: affirmative and negative

1 Read the examples. Complete the rules with the correct form of *be*.

Ernest Shackleton was a great communicator.
Some gladiators were very popular.
Laika wasn't always a celebrity.
Women weren't often gladiators.

1. After *we/you/they*, we use (…) in the affirmative and (…) in the negative.
2. After *I/he/she/it*, we use (…) in the affirmative and (…) in the negative.

2 Complete the sentences with the correct form of *was* or *were*.

1. My favourite programme, *Fame School*, (…) on TV last night. **(+)**
2. Unfortunately, the first performance (…) very good. **(-)**
3. They (…) three brothers from Cardiff. **(+)**
4. The song (…) OK, but their singing (…) ! **(+) (-)**
5. The last performance (…) great and they (…) this week's winners. **(+) (+)**

3 Read the text. Then complete it with *was, were, wasn't* or *weren't*.

The Beatles were an English band in the 1960s and 1970s. Their music **1** (…) new and very different from other music at that time. The four musicians in the band **2** (…) big celebrities in Britain, with lots of fans. Before The Beatles, English music **3** (…) very popular in the USA and British groups **4** (…) very famous. But, with The Beatles, it **5** (…) different. They **6** (…) very popular, with 20 number ones in the USA, and there **7** (…) lots of Beatles fans in America, too. Some people say The Beatles **8** (…) the most important group of all time.

Past simple of *be*: *Yes/No* questions and short answers

4 Read the examples. Choose the correct option to complete the rules.

Were sporting heroes celebrities? Yes, they were.
Was Doug the Pug the first dog in space? No, he wasn't.

1. In questions with *was* and *were*, the verb comes **before/after** the subject.
2. In short answers with *you/we/they*, we use **was(n't)/were(n't)**.
3. In short answers with *I/he/she/it*, we use **was(n't)/were(n't)**.

5 Write questions with *was* and *were*.

1. it / hot / yesterday ? *Was it hot yesterday?*
2. you / 12 / last year ?
3. it / Tuesday / yesterday ?
4. you / at home / at ten o'clock last night ?

Past simple of *be*: *Wh-* questions

6 Read the examples. Order the words to make questions.

Who was the first man on the Moon?
Why were gladiators popular?

When you were seven years old, …

1. best friend / was / who / your ?
2. what / favourite / was / food / your ?
3. was / where / school / your ?
4. teacher's / was / what / your / name ?

7 Work in pairs. Ask and answer the questions in exercise 6.

8 Answer the question to solve the Brain teaser.

BRAIN TEASER

Becky wasn't the photographer. Aaron and Ana were in the middle. Ava wasn't next to Ana.

Can you name the four friends?

Reinforcement and Challenge → Grammar bootcamp pp125–126

Pronunciation: *was*: weak and strong form → p129

Adjectives to describe feelings

1 Read the article. Which sentences 1–5 are true for you?

BEING FAMOUS ON

SOCIAL MEDIA

Most celebrities these days use social media to communicate with their fans. Cristiano Ronaldo and Ariana Grande have each got over 200 million followers on Instagram. Other people become social media stars by posting videos online.

Why do you use social media? And can you live without it?

1 I use social media because I'm **interested** in celebrities.
2 I look at social media when I'm **bored**.
3 I'm **pleased** when my friends 'like' my photos.
4 I feel **worried** if I don't know what my friends are doing.
5 I'm often **tired** because I use social media late at night.

2 Match emojis A–F with the adjectives in the box. There is one extra adjective.

afraid	hungry	ill	relaxed
surprised	thirsty	well	

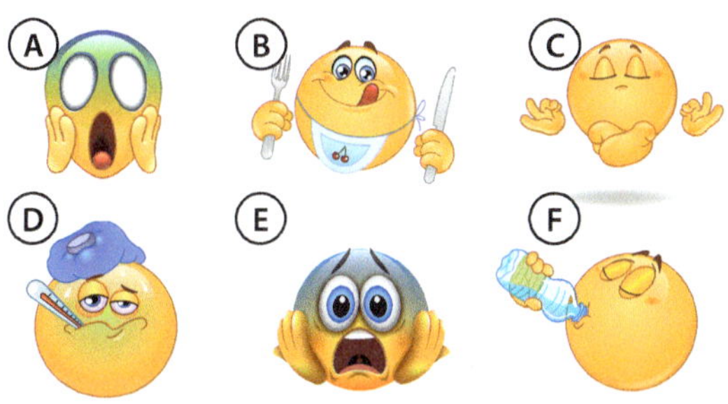

3 Choose the correct option.

1 I drink water when I'm **thirsty/pleased**.
2 People go to the doctor when they're **bored/ill**.
3 Students are often **worried/well** before a test.
4 If you're **hungry/surprised**, have some fruit.
5 I go to bed early when I feel **tired/interested**.

4 Work in pairs. Ask and answer the questions.

1 How do you feel when you … ?
- watch a horror film
- get up in the morning
- pass an exam
- finish school

2 How are you feeling now?

A news report

5 Look at the photo. What does it say about social media? Choose one answer.

a People like social media.
b People on social media aren't real.
c It's better to know people in real life than on social media.

Subskill: Matching speakers with what they say

When you match speakers with what they say, read all the sentences first. Remember, the sentences are not in the same order as you hear them.

6 51 Listen to a news report. Three teens stopped using social media for two weeks. What do they say? Match speakers 1–3 with opinions a–c.

a It was a good experience.
b It was a bad experience.
c Some things were good, but not all.

7 Listen again. Match sentences a–f with speakers 1–3.

Which speaker … ?

a did more things to relax
b thinks that people don't show their real life on social media
c uses social media to organise free-time activities
d wants to stop using social media
e was at home more than usual
f uses social media to find out about friends

8 Work in pairs. Is it a good idea to stop using social media, for example, for one hour a day, or one day a week? Why/Why not?

Past simple of regular verbs: affirmative

1 **Read the examples. Answer the questions.**

> I was happy when the two weeks ended.
> We asked three teenagers to stop using social media.
> She stayed at home a lot of the time.
> I watched TV and played video games.

1 What is the infinitive of the verbs in the examples?
2 What do we add to the verbs when we talk about the past?

2 **Read the Spelling rules on p93. Write the past simple of the verbs in the box.**

> chat decide plan play study walk want

3 **Complete the sentences with the past simple of the verbs in exercise 2.**

1 My brother (…) to stop using social media.
2 We (…) a surprise party for my friend's birthday.
3 I (…) for a test yesterday evening.
4 Last weekend I (…) with my cousin on the phone.
5 My friends and I (…) home after school yesterday.
6 I (…) to be famous when I was younger.
7 We (…) football in the park on Saturday afternoon.

Past simple of irregular verbs: affirmative

4 **Some verbs are irregular in the past simple. Read the examples and write the past simple of verbs 1–4.**

> My friends went to the party without me.
> I had more free time. I did my homework.
> I met my friends, and we chatted face to face.

1 have 2 meet 3 do 4 go

5 **Rewrite the sentences. Change the verbs from the present simple to the past simple. Use the Irregular verb list on pp134–135 to help you.**

1 My friends take a lot of photos.
2 Some people become famous on social media.
3 I get up late on Saturday morning.
4 Ben meets his classmates after school.
5 We go to a café on Friday evening.
6 I see a basketball match at the weekend.

6 **Write two sentences about what you did …**

1 last Saturday 2 last week 3 last year

7 **Work in pairs. Compare with a partner. Are any things the same?**

I played video games last Saturday.

Me too. And I got up late.

8 **Choose the correct option.**

GRAMMAR ROUND-UP

1 2 3 4 5 6 7 **8**

A statue for Mary Anning

Mary Anning **1 was/were** the first woman palaeontologist in the UK. She **2 study/studied** fossils in her hometown of Lyme Regis in the 1800s, but it **3 isn't/wasn't** possible for women at that time to be scientists. Today, most people **4 doesn't/don't** know her name.

But 11-year-old Evie Swire **5 want/wants** to change that. The British schoolgirl is also from Lyme Regis. **6 There isn't/There aren't** a statue for Mary Anning in the town, and Evie **7 is/are** collecting money to make one. Evie is **8 more young/younger** than her hero, but she also collects fossils.

You can **9 find out/to find out** more about Evie Swire online. There are **10 a lot of/any** websites about her campaign.

Research

Find out one fact about Evie Swire or about Mary Anning.

Reinforcement and Challenge → Grammar bootcamp p126

Talking about last weekend

1 **Work in pairs. Which activities do you usually do at the weekend? When do you do them?**

do homework   go shopping   go to the cinema
have a piano lesson   play basketball
play video games   stay at home   watch TV

2 **Watch the video. Do the friends talk about their real weekend or an imaginary one?**

3 **Watch the video again. Number the Key phrases in the order you hear them.**

4 **Complete the dialogue with the Key phrases.**

Eddie: Hi! **1** (…) your weekend?

Kelly: It **2** (…), thanks. Saturday, I went shopping with Taylor Swift.

Eddie: Really?

Kelly: Yes, and that night, we **3** (…) to a party.

Eddie: **4** (…) fun?

Kelly: Yes, it was. I had a **5** (…)! Lots of famous people were there.

Eddie: **6** (…) Sunday?

Kelly: Sunday, I went to the movies with Finn Wolfhard. What about you?

Eddie: Well, Saturday, **7** (…) basketball for the Lakers.

Kelly: With LeBron James?

Eddie: That's right. Then Sunday, **8** (…) Zac Efron to play video games.

Kelly: Really?

Eddie: No, not really … Back to reality!

5 **Create your own dialogue. Follow the steps in the Skills boost.**

SKILLS BOOST

THINK

Work individually. Copy and complete the table with activities and who you did them with. You can invent activities and people, or talk about real ones.

Friday evening	Saturday	Sunday
watched TV		

PREPARE

Work in pairs. Write your dialogue. Use Key phrases to ask and talk about last weekend.

Hi … How was your weekend?

PRACTISE

Practise your dialogue.

PERFORM

Act out your dialogue for the class.

6 **Peer review** **Listen to your classmates and answer the questions.**

1 Are any of the activities the same as yours?
2 Do they use the Key phrases correctly?

Key phrases

Asking about last weekend:

How was your weekend?
What about in the evening/Sunday?
Was it fun?

Talking about last weekend:

It was great/fun/good/awesome/OK, thanks.
We went …   I played …   I met …
I had a great time!

US → UK

I went to the movies. (US) → I went to the cinema. (UK)
What about Sunday? (US) → What about on Sunday? (UK)

JEAN GREY

(1) My favourite character is Jean Grey, or the Dark Phoenix. She's a superhero in the *X-Men* films. She knows what people are thinking, and she can also move objects with her mind.

(2) Jean was born in New Jersey. Her father was a teacher, and her mother worked in a restaurant. When she was eight, the family had a car accident and Jean's sister died. After the accident, Jean's psychic powers started to appear, but she was unhappy at home, and she also had problems at school. Her parents sent her to a hospital. There, she met Professor Charles Xavier. The professor helped her, and she went to study at the Xavier Institute, a school for X-Men.

(3) I like Jean Grey because she's strong, and she's also a good person. Her friends are important to her, and she always tries to help people.

A description of a fictional character

1 Read about a favourite fictional character. Answer the questions.

1 Who is the character? What film, book or TV series is she from?
2 Why does the writer like her?

2 Read the description again and complete the sentences.

1 Jean Grey is from (...) .
2 Her family had an accident when (...) .
3 Her psychic powers started to appear after (...) .
4 Her parents sent her to a hospital because (...) .
5 She got better because (...) .
6 When she left the hospital, she (...) .
7 At the school, she learned to become one of the (...) .

3 Match paragraphs 1–3 in the description with information a–c.

a family and early life
b why I like this fictional character
c the name of the character and general information

Subskill: *also*

We use *also* to add another idea or fact to one before.

4 Find three sentences with *also* in the description. Choose the correct option to complete the rules.

1 *Also* comes **before/after** the verb *be*.
2 *Also* comes **before/after** other verbs.
3 *Also* comes **before *can*/between *can* and the verb.**

Writing competence → Workbook pp120–121

5 **Rewrite the sentences with *also*. Then match the sentences with the characters in the box.**

Jack Sparrow   Katniss Everdeen   Lisa Simpson
Sherlock Holmes   Thor

1 He's strong. He can fly.
2 He was born on a ship. He became a pirate.
3 He's intelligent and he's a good detective.
4 She knows a lot about nature and she can climb trees.
5 She plays the saxophone and she's very intelligent.

6 **Write a description of your favourite fictional character. Follow the steps in the Skills boost.**

SKILLS BOOST

THINK

1 Choose your favourite fictional character from a film, book or TV series.
2 Make notes about the character. (You can use the internet to help you.) Think about:
- general information about the character
- family
- the story of his/her early life
- why you like him/her

PREPARE

Organise your notes into three paragraphs.
Include at least one example of *also*.

WRITE

Write about your favourite fictional character.
My favourite fictional character is …

CHECK

Read your description and answer the questions.
1 Do you have three paragraphs?
2 Do you use the past simple correctly?
3 Do you use *also* in the correct position in a sentence?

7 **Peer review** **Work in groups. Read your classmates' descriptions. Answer the questions.**

1 What information is new for you?
2 Does the writer use the past simple correctly?
3 Does the writer use *also* correctly?

QUICK REVIEW 7

Grammar

Past simple of *be*

The past of the verb *be* is *was/were, wasn't/weren't*.
I/He/She/It was/wasn't   You/We/They were/weren't
*Laika **was** a dog from Russia.*
*Singers **weren't** on social media a hundred years ago.*
To make a question, we use (question word) + *was/were*.
***Was** Grace Hopper a celebrity?*   *Yes, she **was**.*
***Were** The Beatles from London?*   *No, they **weren't**.*
***Where were** you yesterday?*

Past simple of regular verbs: affirmative

We use the past simple to talk about finished actions in the past.
To make the past simple of regular verbs, add *-ed*.
*I watch**ed** TV yesterday.*
*We play**ed** video games last Saturday.*

Spelling rules

1 most verbs, add *-ed*
*walk → walk**ed***   *look → look**ed***
2 when the verb ends in *-e*, add *-d*
*change → change**d***   *dance → dance**d***
3 when the verb ends in consonant + *-y*, omit *-y* and add *-ied*
*study → stud**ied***   *carry → carr**ied***
4 when the verb ends in one vowel + one consonant, double the final consonant and add *-ed*
*stop → stop**ped***   *chat → chat**ted***

Past simple of irregular verbs: affirmative

Some verbs are irregular in the past simple.
*go → **went***   *have → **had***   *do → **did***
*see → **saw***   *take → **took***   *meet → **met***
*I **went** to the cinema last weekend. I **saw** a good film.*

Vocabulary

52 Jobs

actor, artist, astronaut, cook, doctor, farmer, inventor, singer, teacher, waiter

53 Dates

January, February, March, April, May, June, July, August, September, October, November, December
first, second, third, fourth, fifth, sixth, seventh, eighth, ninth, tenth, eleventh, twelfth, thirteenth, fourteenth, fifteenth, sixteenth, seventeenth, eighteenth, nineteenth, twentieth, twenty-first, twenty-second, twenty-third, twenty-fourth, twenty-fifth, twenty-sixth, twenty-seventh, twenty-eighth, twenty-ninth, thirtieth, thirty-first

54 Adjectives to describe feelings

afraid, bored, hungry, ill, interested, pleased, relaxed, surprised, thirsty, tired, well, worried

7 Project

WDYT? (What do you think?)

What does it mean to be famous?

TASK: Make a comic about an unknown hero.

Learning outcomes

1 I can produce and present a comic.
2 I can research and decide what to include.
3 I can use appropriate language from the unit.

Graphic organiser → Project planner p133

1 Watch a video of students reading their classmates' comic. Why is Elizabeth Blackwell a hero?

STEP 1: THINK

2 Read the students' notes. Which information is not in the comic in the Model project?

ELIZABETH BLACKWELL
03.02.1821 (Bristol, UK) – 31.05.1910 (Hastings, UK)
Personal: sister, Emily / education = important / → USA 1832
Professional: teacher / studied medicine, other students & teachers unfriendly / opened two hospitals & a medical school

3 Why is the text written in the first person (*I*)?

4 How do the pictures help us understand the story?

STEP 2: PLAN

5 Work in pairs. Choose an unknown hero for your project. Find your own hero or choose one of the people in the box.

Annie Londonderry (traveller)
Francisco Javier de Balmis (doctor)
Michael Collins (astronaut)
Rachel Carson (biologist)

6 Research your hero and make notes.

7 Work in pairs. Read the tips in the Super skills box and practise saying the Key phrases with a partner.

COLLABORATION SUPER SKILLS

Researching information and deciding what to include

Tips

Discuss all your ideas before you decide.
Include surprising or interesting information.
Say why the person is an unknown hero.

Key phrases

OK, so what information have we got?
What information do you think is important?
Shall we include … ?
I think/don't think (…) is very important.
OK great, that's six points.

8 Work together to choose the six most important points to include. Use the tips and Key phrases in the Super skills box.

STEP 3: CREATE

9 Read the *How to …* tips on p133 and prepare your comic. You can draw it yourself or use an online comic creating tool.

Grammar and Vocabulary → Quick review p93

Model project

Elizabeth Blackwell: doctor

STEP 4: PRESENT

10 **Exchange your comic with another pair.**

11 **Peer review** **As you read your classmates' comic, answer the questions.**

1. Is the person a good example of an unknown hero? Why?
2. Is the comic clear and attractive?
3. Does it include important information about the person's life?

7 FINAL REFLECTION

1. **The task**
   Is your comic clear and attractive?
2. **Super skill**
   Do you choose interesting information? Give examples.
3. **Language**
   In your comic, do you use language from the unit? Give examples.

8 From A to B

WDYT? (What do you think?)

What's the best way to travel, and why?

TRAVEL ALONE OR TRAVEL TOGETHER?

Vocabulary: transport; transport collocations

Grammar: past simple (negative, questions and short answers); superlative adjectives

Reading: a magazine article and Q & A interview about scooters in the 21st century

Listening: a radio programme about Bike to School Week

Speaking: buying a ticket

Writing: a story

Project: do a class survey about transport and present the results

Video skills p97

Real-world speaking p103

Project pp106–107

Transport

1 **Match the words in the box with photos A–G.**

bike boat bus car plane taxi train

2 **Work in pairs. Answer the questions.**

1 When do you use the types of transport in exercise 1?

2 Is it better to travel alone or together? Why?

When do you travel by car?

On Saturdays, when I go to football. What about you?

Language note

We use the preposition *by* to talk about ways to travel.

*I go to school **by** bus. I never travel **by** taxi.*

But we say *on foot*.

*I come to school **on foot**. = I walk to school.*

3 Match the definitions with the words in the box.

ambulance ~~coach~~ helicopter lorry motorbike scooter ship tram underground

1 It's a type of bus. It takes people from one city to another. *coach*
2 This takes people to and from hospital.
3 It's faster than a bike because it's got an engine.
4 This is the system of trains that travel under a city.
5 It travels on roads and carries things, e.g. food, cars.
6 It's usually smaller than a plane, but it also travels in the air.
7 It's got two wheels and you move it with your foot.
8 It's bigger than a boat. It carries people or things.
9 It's similar to a train but travels on streets in a city.

4 Write types of transport. Use words from exercises 1 and 3.

1 four ways to travel between cities
2 three types of transport with two wheels
3 three types of public transport in a city
4 two types of transport that travel on water
5 two types of transport that travel in the air

5 Complete the sentences with the words in the box.

driver journey passenger pilot ticket travelcard

1 A (...) drives a bus or car.
2 A (...) flies a plane.
3 A (...) travels in a car, bus or plane but doesn't drive.
4 A (...) is when you go from one place to another.
5 You buy a (...) to travel on public transport.
6 You buy a (...) when you use a bus or train more than one time.

6 Work in pairs. Answer the questions.

1 How long is your journey to school?
2 When you travel by bus, do you buy a ticket or a travelcard? Why?
3 The last time you travelled by car, who was the driver?

VIDEO SKILLS

7 Watch the video. What country does Nadiya visit? Why does she go there?

8 Work in pairs. Answer the questions.

1 Nadiya visits the city and the countryside. How are they different?
2 Why do people watch programmes like this?
3 This video is a documentary. How is it different to a vlog? Think about photos, music, graphics, etc.

A magazine article and Q & A interview

1 **Read the clues and solve the puzzles.**

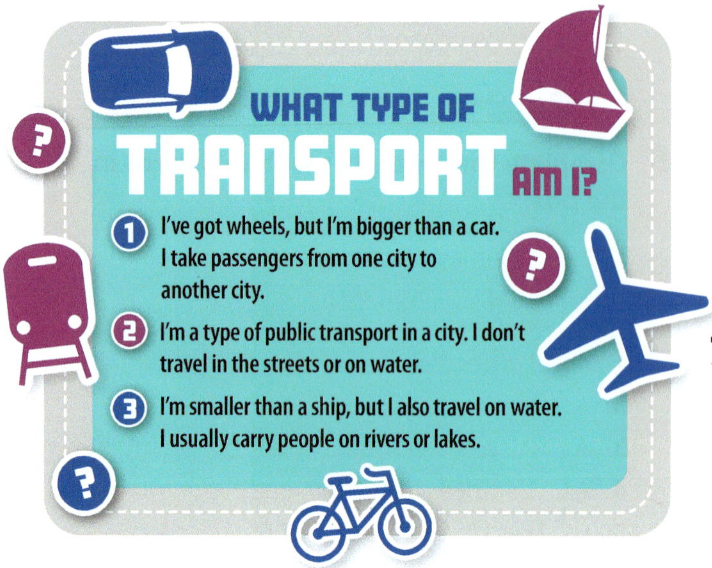

2 **Work in pairs. Take turns to describe a type of transport. Can your partner guess which one you are?**

I've got two wheels. I'm faster than a bike.

Are you a motorbike?

Yes, I am.

3 **Look at the photos in the article. What type of transport can you see? What do people use it for?**

Subskill: Asking questions before you read

Before you read, ask yourself questions, e.g. *What do I want to know?* This helps you to read actively.

4 55 **What would you like to know about scooters? Write a question. Then read and listen to the article to see if you find the answer to your question.**

5 **Read the first text again. Answer the questions.**

1 How old are scooters?
2 Who made the first scooters, and why?
3 Why did Wim Ouboter make a scooter?
4 Why were Razor scooters better than other scooters?
5 Where did scooters first become popular as a type of transport?
6 Why is riding a scooter good for your health?

6 **Read the second text again. Are the sentences true or false? Give reasons for your answers.**

1 Razor made scooters because they wanted to start a new sport.
2 They organised a competition for riders to do tricks.
3 The company puts videos online to help people learn tricks.
4 Funk Bros are celebrities because they write a blog about scooters.
5 Millions of people watch videos of tricks online.
6 Scooter riding is an Olympic sport.

7 **Word work** **Match the definitions to the words in bold in the text.**

1 an event where people try to be more successful or better than other people
2 something that suddenly becomes very popular
3 children or young people (informal)
4 things you do with a skateboard or scooter, etc. in a clever way
5 cars, buses, etc. on the road at the same time
6 a form of something that is a little different from another form

8 **Complete the sentences with words from exercise 7.**

1 A lot of (…) at my school have got a scooter.
2 K-pop is a recent (…) .
3 People practise a lot before they can do a (…) on a skateboard.
4 I was late for school because there was a lot of (…) .
5 I preferred the film (…) to the book.
6 Our school organised a (…) to see who can make the best robot.

CRITICAL THINKING

SUPER SKILLS

1 **Remember** Look at the article again. What are the advantages of scooters as a type of transport? Can you think of any disadvantages? Think about these adjectives:

safe/dangerous cheap/expensive
comfortable/uncomfortable

2 **Apply** Choose two of the types of transport in the box. Think of two advantages and two disadvantages of each.

bike bus taxi tram underground

3 **Create** Think of three ways to make the transport system better where you live. Then choose the best way.

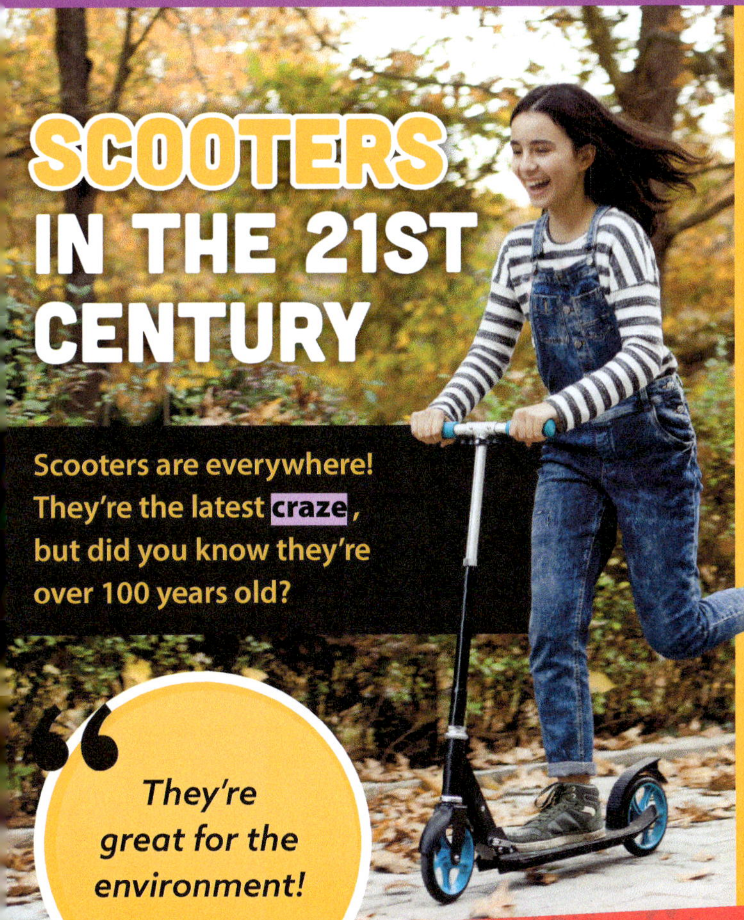

SCOOTERS IN THE 21ST CENTURY

Scooters are everywhere! They're the latest **craze**, but did you know they're over 100 years old?

> *They're great for the environment!*

That's right! Kids made the first scooters as toys in about 1910, but they didn't become popular until later. In 1997, a Swiss businessman called Wim Ouboter invented a modern version of the scooter to go to his favourite shop when he didn't want to drive.

Then in the 2000s, a company called Razor made cheaper and lighter scooters. Japanese businessmen in Tokyo started using them on their journey to work. Soon, scooters were common in other cities too.

Why? Well, scooters are faster in **traffic** than cars. You can also carry them on a bus or train. Riding a scooter is good exercise – and they're great for the environment!

A new EXTREME SPORT!

Go to any skate park and you can see kids riding scooters. In fact, it's the latest extreme sport!

How did it start?
When Razor made their first scooters in the 2000s, they didn't plan to start a sport. But kids soon realised the scooters were great for doing **tricks**. The company decided to organise a **competition**, and now there's a scooter world championship.

Why did it become popular?
The internet helped to make the sport popular. Riders post videos online and other people can learn their tricks. Millions of people watch the videos of celebrity riders the Funk Bros.

What about the future?
Many people want to see scooters in the X Games and in the Olympics. But for now, it's just a cool sport!

fun facts
Mared Jelinka travelled from New Delhi in India to Malaysia on his scooter. It took seven months, and he collected money to pay a teacher for children in Bangladesh for one year.

The longer read → Resource centre

Past simple: negative

1 Read the examples. Answer the questions.

Scooters didn't become popular until later.
He didn't want to drive.
I didn't know that scooters were old.

1 What word do we use to make a negative past simple?
2 What form of the verb do we use after this word?

2 Rewrite the sentences so that they are correct for the year 1910. Make the verbs negative.

1 Children **used** scooters as transport.
In 1910, children didn't use scooters as transport.
2 People **travelled** a lot by plane.
3 Children **went** to school by bus.
4 Most cities **had** an underground.
5 You **saw** a lot of cars in the streets.
6 Teens **did** sport on skateboards.

Language note

We often use the past simple with past time expressions: *yesterday, last weekend, last year, a month ago, a hundred years ago.*

3 Complete the sentences with the affirmative or negative form of the verbs so they are true for you.

1 I (...) to school this morning. **(walk)**
2 I (...) by plane last year. **(travel)**
3 I (...) basketball last Saturday. **(play)**
4 I (...) to the cinema last weekend. **(go)**
5 I (...) before eight o'clock yesterday. **(get up)**

Past simple: questions and short answers

4 Read the examples. Choose the correct option to complete the rules.

Did you know that scooters are over a hundred years old? Yes, I did./No, I didn't.
How did it start? Why did it become popular?

1 In past simple *Yes/No* questions, we use (...) + subject + (...) .
2 In short answers, we use *Yes* + subject + (...) (affirmative) or *No* + subject + (...) (negative).
3 For *Wh-* questions, we use question word + (...) + (...) + infinitive.

5 Order the words to make questions.

1 you / watch TV / did / yesterday evening ?
2 how / today / to school / you / did / come ?
3 did / any homework / do / you / last weekend ?
4 did / last night / have / you / for dinner / what ?
5 you / did / when / your best friend / meet ?
6 do / did / what / last weekend / you ?

6 Answer the questions in exercise 5 so they are true for you.

7 Complete the text with the past simple form of the verbs in brackets.

History blog Login

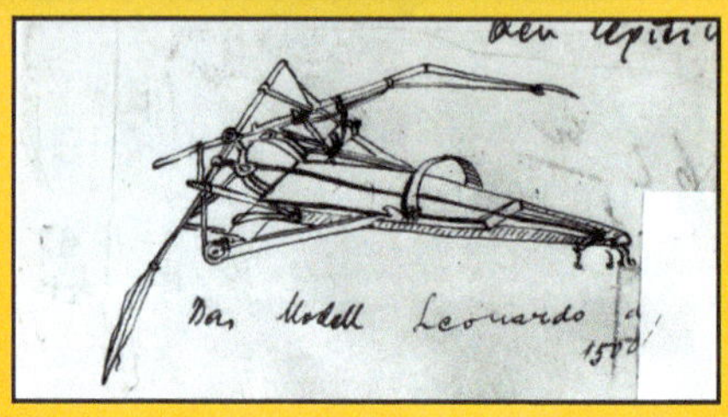

Leonardo da Vinci's transport ideas

Leonardo was a famous artist, but **1** (...) **(you / know)** that he also invented things? He **2** (...) **(design)** a car, a plane and a helicopter. He **3** (...) **(not make)** these things, but he **4** (...) **(draw)** pictures of them. The first plane **5** (...) **(not fly)** until 1906, but da Vinci **6** (...) **(study)** birds to get ideas for his flying machine. He also **7** (...) **(imagine)** a helicopter many years before the first flight. When **8** (...) **(he / live)**? Well, we don't know exactly, but probably between 1452 and 1519. He **9** (...) **(not know)** that one day his ideas would become a reality!

8 Answer the question to solve the Brain teaser.

BRAIN TEASER

A bus driver went the wrong way on a one-way street, but the police didn't stop him. Why not?

Reinforcement and Challenge → Grammar bootcamp pp126–127
Pronunciation: Contracted forms → p129

Transport collocations

1 **Look at part of a travel app. Use a verb from box A and a phrase from box B to make transport collocations.**

A drive go ride take travel

B a bike a car by plane on foot the train/bus

2 **Use the irregular verbs list on pp134–135 to check if the verbs in Box A are regular or irregular in the past. Then complete the sentences.**

1 I *rode my bike to school* yesterday.
2 I (...) yesterday.
3 I (...) last weekend.
4 I (...) last year.

3 **Complete the collocations with the words in the box.**

a bus a taxi a ticket get into/out of go ring the road trains wait

1 cross (...)

2 buy (...)

3 change (...)

4 (...) on a tour

5 (...) in a queue

6 (...) the bell

7 take (...)

8 get on/off (...)

9 (...) a car

4 **Work in pairs. Order the actions in exercise 3 that you do ...**

1 on your journey to school
2 on the journey from your home to the centre of your city
3 when you go shopping

A radio programme

5 **Work in pairs. Describe the photo.**

1 What can you see?
2 Where are they going?
3 How do you know?

Subskill: Listening to choose the best summary

First, read the options. When you listen, try to understand the general meaning; don't worry about understanding every word.

6 56 **Listen to a radio interview and choose the best summary.**

The programme is about ...

a an Olympic cyclist who cycled to school as a child
b a special week to get more teenagers to cycle to school
c a doctor who wants teenagers to do more sport

7 **Listen again and complete the sentences with information from the radio interview.**

1 3rd–7th June is (...) .
2 Isla Graham is the (...) .
3 The most popular transport for Fisher Valley High School students is the (...) .
4 Many teenagers don't do (...) .
5 Cycling helps students stay healthy and it's also lots of (...) .
6 Cycling is also good for the (...) .

8 **Work in pairs. Discuss the questions.**

1 Do you cycle to school? Why/Why not?
2 Would you like to take part in this event?

Research

What percentage of teenagers cycle to school in your country? Is there a Bike to School Week where you live?

Vocabulary extension → Workbook p107

Superlative adjectives

1 Read the examples. Choose the correct option to complete the rules.

> … the fastest person at the Olympics …
> … one of the most popular sporting heroes …
> Cycling is one of the healthiest ways to get to school.
> It's the least negative form of transport for the environment.
> That's one of the biggest advantages. That's the best thing about cycling.

1. We use superlative adjectives to compare **two/three or more** things.
2. Before superlative adjectives, we use ***the/more***.
3. The opposite of *most* is ***less/least***.

2 Copy and complete the table with superlative adjectives.

Adjective	Superlative
fast	**1** *the fastest*
big	**2** (…)
healthy	**3** (…)
popular	**4** (…)
dangerous	**5** (…)
good	**6** (…)
bad	**7** *the worst*

3 Match rules a–e with adjectives 1–5 in exercise 2.

a Two-syllable adjectives ending in *-y* → *-~~y~~ the* + *-iest*.
b One-syllable adjectives → *the* + *-est*.
c Adjectives with two or more syllables → *the most/the least* + adjective.
d Some adjectives are irregular in the superlative form.
e One-syllable adjectives ending in consonant + vowel + consonant (except *-w*) → *the* + double the final consonant + *-est*.

4 Write the superlative form of the adjectives in the box.

> ~~expensive~~ heavy hot interesting light slow small thin thirsty

expensive – the most expensive

5 Complete the questions with the correct superlative form of the adjectives in brackets.

1. What's (…) **(fast)** type of transport in your city?
2. What's (…) **(popular)** place to go at the weekend?
3. What's (…) **(famous)** sports stadium?
4. Where's (…) **(good)** place for tourists to stay?
5. Where are (…) **(expensive)** shops?
6. What's (…) **(cheap)** place for teenagers to eat?

6 Answer the questions in exercise 5 so they are true for you. Then ask and answer the questions in pairs.

7 Choose the correct option.

GRAMMAR ROUND-UP

1 2 3 4 5 6 7 8

IS IT A PLANE? IS IT A CAR?

THE ANSWER IS YES TO BOTH!

For years, a flying car **1** (…) something people **2** (…) about in books. You didn't **3** (…) them on the roads or in the sky. But now you can **4** (…) the Terrafugia TF-X – the world's first flying car. The TF-X **5** (…) on the road like a car, goes into the air like a helicopter and **6** (…) like a plane. It can travel up to 640 km and it **7** (…) a top speed of 160 km per hour. At a price of $400,000, it isn't the **8** (…) way to travel. But with no waiting at airports or sitting in traffic on busy roads, it's certainly one of **9** (…) .

	a	b	c
1	**a** be	**b** was	**c** were
2	**a** read	**b** did read	**c** reads
3	**a** saw not	**b** saw	**c** see
4	**a** to buy	**b** buy	**c** buying
5	**a** drive	**b** drives	**c** driving
6	**a** flying	**b** flies	**c** fly
7	**a** 's got	**b** have got	**c** got
8	**a** more cheap	**b** cheaper	**c** cheapest
9	**a** the easiest	**b** the most easy	**c** the easier

Reinforcement and Challenge → Grammar bootcamp p127

Buying a ticket

1 **Read the definitions and watch the video. What type of ticket does Nadia buy?**

a a single: a ticket for one journey

b a return: a ticket to go to a place and come back

c a travelcard: a ticket to travel as much as you want in a period of time

2 **Watch again. Which two Key phrases do you not hear?**

3 **Complete the dialogue with the Key phrases. Watch again and check.**

Clerk: Good morning. Can I help you?

Nadia: Hello. Yes, I want to go to Liverpool, please. What's the fastest **1** (…) ?

Clerk: Let's see … **2** (…) the 10:15 train to Birmingham and **3** (…) there.

Nadia: OK, fine. How much **4** (…) ?

Clerk: Is that single or **5** (…) ?

Nadia: Return, please.

Clerk: That's £40, please. There's a train **6** (…) .

Nadia: Here you are. Where do I **7** (…) ?

Clerk: Platform 2.

Nadia: Thanks. Have a nice day.

Clerk: You too.

4 **Create your own dialogue. Follow the steps in the Skills boost.**

SKILLS BOOST

THINK

Think of a place to go. Then make notes. Use your imagination.

- Going to
- Single/Return
- Next train
- From
- Instructions

PREPARE

Prepare a dialogue with the help of the information above. Use Key phrases for asking for information and giving instructions and information.

Good morning. Can I help you?

PRACTISE

Practise your dialogue.

PERFORM

Act out your dialogue for the class.

5 **Peer review** **Listen to your classmates and answer the questions.**

1 Where is the passenger going and how much does a ticket cost?

2 Which Key phrases do they use?

Key phrases

Asking for information:

What's the fastest way?
What time's the next train?
How much does it cost?
Is that single or return?
Where do I get the train?

Giving instructions and information:

Take the (10:15) train.
Buy your ticket (at the machine).
Change trains (at Birmingham).
There's a train in (five) minutes.

Real-world grammar

What's the fastest way?

CALLING ALL TRAVELLERS!

In this month's competition, we want to hear about **your best or worst journey**. Did you have a fantastic trip and meet amazing people? Or did everything go wrong? Tell us the story of your journey in 120–150 words, and you could win a helicopter ride for two people.

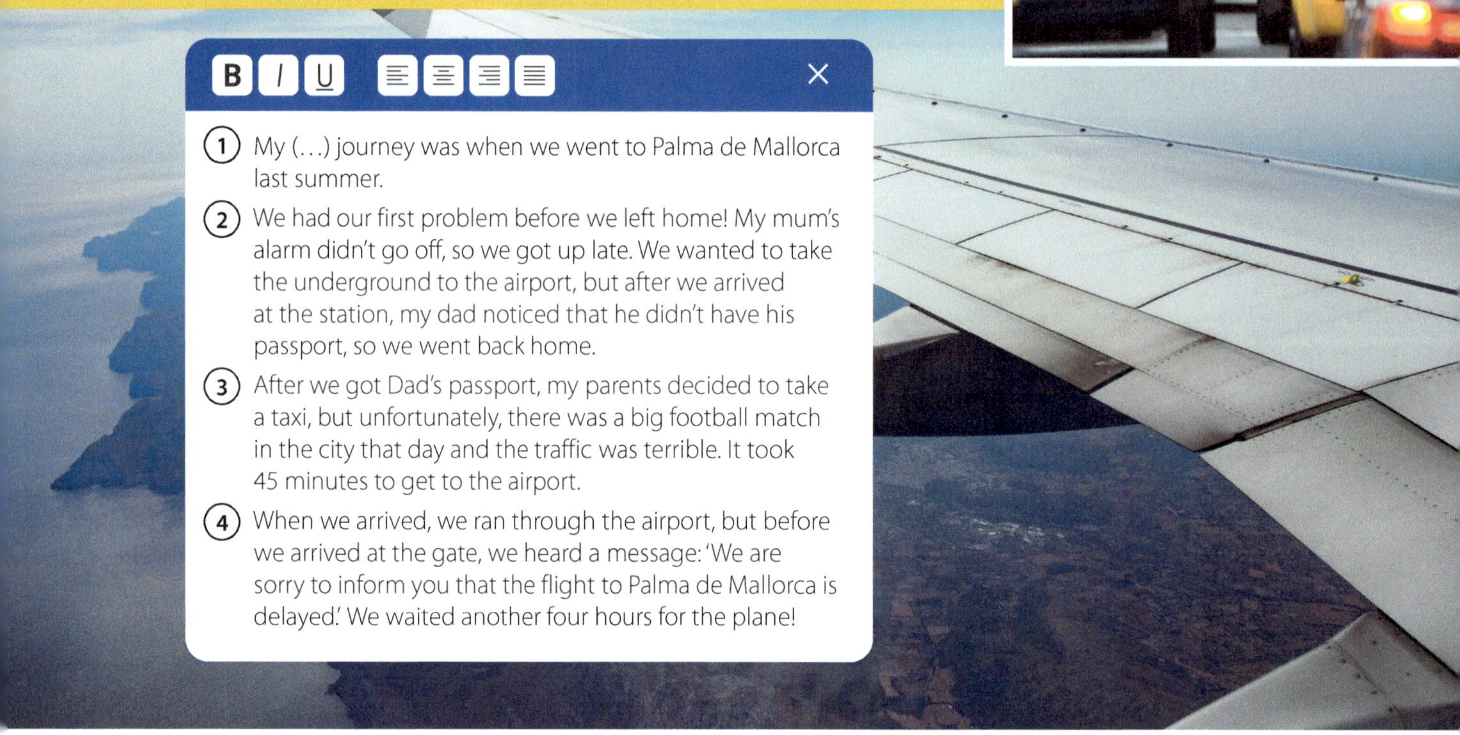

(1) My (...) journey was when we went to Palma de Mallorca last summer.

(2) We had our first problem before we left home! My mum's alarm didn't go off, so we got up late. We wanted to take the underground to the airport, but after we arrived at the station, my dad noticed that he didn't have his passport, so we went back home.

(3) After we got Dad's passport, my parents decided to take a taxi, but unfortunately, there was a big football match in the city that day and the traffic was terrible. It took 45 minutes to get to the airport.

(4) When we arrived, we ran through the airport, but before we arrived at the gate, we heard a message: 'We are sorry to inform you that the flight to Palma de Mallorca is delayed.' We waited another four hours for the plane!

A story

1 **Read the advert for a competition. Then work in pairs. Tell your partner about it in your own words.**

2 **Read the travel story. Is it about the writer's best or worst journey?**

3 **There are four paragraphs. Copy and complete the table with a description of each paragraph.**

Paragraph 1	*introduction*
Paragraph 2	
Paragraph 3	
Paragraph 4	

4 **Read the story again. Order the events.**

a Dad noticed he didn't have his passport.
b Mum's alarm didn't go off.
c We arrived at the airport.
d We heard a message about the delay.
e We went home again.
f We waited for the plane.
g We arrived at the station.

Subskill: *before* and *after*

We use *before* and *after* to show the order of events.

5 **Read the examples with *before* and *after* and say what happened first: a or b.**

1 Before we arrived at the gate, we heard a message.
  a We arrived. **b** We heard a message.

2 After we arrived at the station, my dad noticed that he didn't have his passport.
  a We arrived. **b** Dad noticed he didn't have his passport.

Writing competence → Workbook pp122–123

6 Find one more example with *before* and one more example with *after* in the text. Identify the first event in each case.

7 Connect the sentences with *before* or *after*.

a **1** We got a bus.
2 We took the train. **(before)**
Before we took the train, we got a bus.

b **1** My friend arrived.
2 We watched a film. **(after)**

c **1** I had a shower.
2 I had breakfast. **(before)**

d **1** I had a piano lesson.
2 I did my homework. **(after)**

e **1** We visited Rome.
2 We went to Sicily. **(before)**

8 Write your story for the competition. Follow the steps in the Skills boost.

SKILLS BOOST

THINK

1 Think of a real journey or invent one.
2 Make notes about what happened.

PREPARE

Organise your notes into logical paragraphs for different parts of the story.

WRITE

Write your story. Use the story in exercise 2 to help you.
My best/worst journey was …

CHECK

Read your competition entry. Answer the questions.
1 Do you use the past simple correctly?
2 Do you use *before* and *after* to show the order things happened?
3 Is your story interesting? Why?

9 **Peer review** Work in groups. Read your classmates' stories and answer the questions.
1 Does the writer use the past simple correctly?
2 Does the writer order events with *before* and *after*?
3 Which story is the best? Why?

QUICK REVIEW 8

Grammar

Past simple: negative, questions and short answers

To form the negative, we use *didn't* (*did not*) + infinitive.
*They **didn't come** by car.*
To form *Yes/No* questions, we use *Did* + subject + infinitive?
Short answers: *Yes,* + subject + *did.*/*No,* + subject + *didn't.*
To form *Wh-* questions, use question word + *did* + subject + infinitive?
***Did** you buy the tickets?* *Yes, I **did**.*
*When **did** you buy them?*

Superlative adjectives

To form the superlative form of an adjective, we use *(one of) the* + superlative adjective.
One-syllable adjectives → *the* + *-est*
old → ***the** old**est***
One-syllable adjectives ending in consonant + vowel + consonant (except *-w*) → *the* + double the final consonant + *-est*
thin → ***the** thin**nest***
Two-syllable adjectives ending in *-y* → ~~*-y*~~ *the* + *-iest*
happy → ***the** happ**iest***
Adjectives with two or more syllables → *the most/the least* + adjective
expensive → ***the most/least** expensive*
Some adjectives are irregular in the superlative form.
good → ***the best*** *bad* → ***the worst***

Vocabulary

57 Transport

ambulance, bike, boat, bus, car, coach, driver, helicopter, journey, lorry, motorbike, passenger, pilot, plane, scooter, ship, taxi, ticket, train, tram, travelcard, underground

58 Transport collocations

buy a ticket, change trains, cross the road, drive a car, get into/out of a car, get on/off a bus, go on a tour, go on foot, ride a bike, ring the bell, take a taxi, take the train/bus, travel by plane, wait in a queue

8 Project

WDYT? (What do you think?)

What's the best way to travel, and why?

TASK: Do a class survey about transport and present the results.

Learning outcomes

1 I can design a survey, ask my classmates questions and report the results.

2 I can decide on different roles in groupwork.

3 I can use appropriate language from the unit.

Graphic organiser → Project planner p133

1 Watch a video of students presenting their survey results. What is the most popular type of transport to go on holiday?

STEP 1: THINK

2 Look at the students' survey in the Model project. Answer the questions.

1 How many questions are there?
2 Is there space to write the answers?
3 Are there questions in the past simple and present simple?

3 Think of two more questions to ask in the survey.

STEP 2: PLAN

4 Work in groups of three. Prepare a transport survey.

- Write at least three questions.
- Include space to write the answers.
- Make sure that each person in the group has got a copy of the survey.

5 Ask other students in the class your questions. Each student in your group asks four other students. Remember to write the answers.

STEP 3: CREATE

6 Look at the results of the survey in the Model project. How do the students present their results for each question: a bar chart or a pie chart?

7 Read the tips in the Super skills box and practise saying the Key phrases with your group.

COLLABORATION — SUPER SKILLS

Deciding on roles in groupwork

Tips

Make a list of things to do.
Decide who can do each thing.
Check to see that you divide the work equally.

Key phrases

What are the things to do?
We can do this part together.
I can make a pie chart for question one.
How can we divide the presentation?
Why don't we each … ?

8 Read the *How to …* tips on p133. Then prepare a presentation of the results of your survey. Use the tips and Key phrases in the Super skills box.

9 Practise your presentation in your group.

Grammar and Vocabulary → Quick review p105

Model project

Transport survey

1 How do you come to school?

2 What other types of transport do you use?

- bus
- underground
- bike
- tram
- other

3 How did you travel on holiday last year?

- plane
- car
- train
- coach

Transport to school

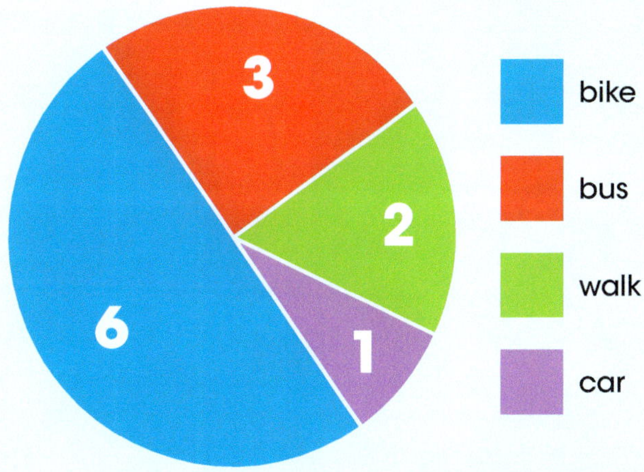

Transport for last holiday

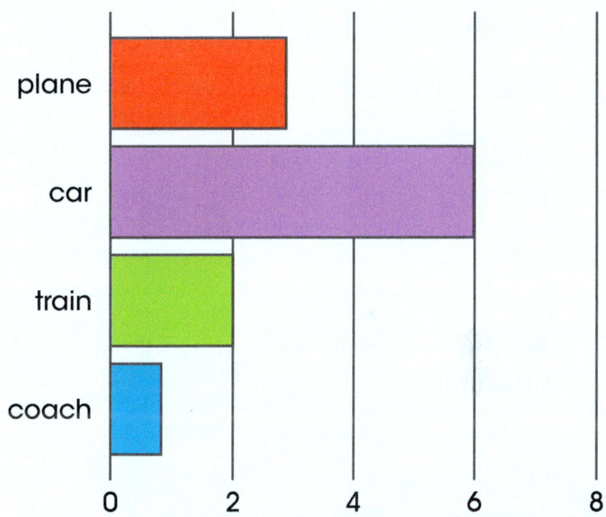

Other types of transport used

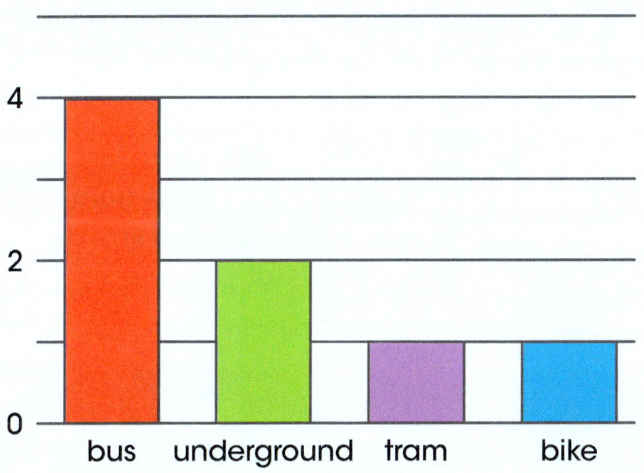

STEP 4: PRESENT

10 **Present the results of your survey to the class.**

11 **Peer review** **As you listen to your classmates, answer the questions.**

1. Are the results of the survey similar to yours?
2. Do you agree with the conclusion?

8 FINAL REFLECTION

1 The task

Did you include three or more questions in your survey?

Did you present your results clearly, and end with a conclusion?

2 Super skill

Did everyone in the group take a different role? Give examples.

3 Language

In your survey and presentation, did you use language from the unit? Give examples.

9 Look what you know!

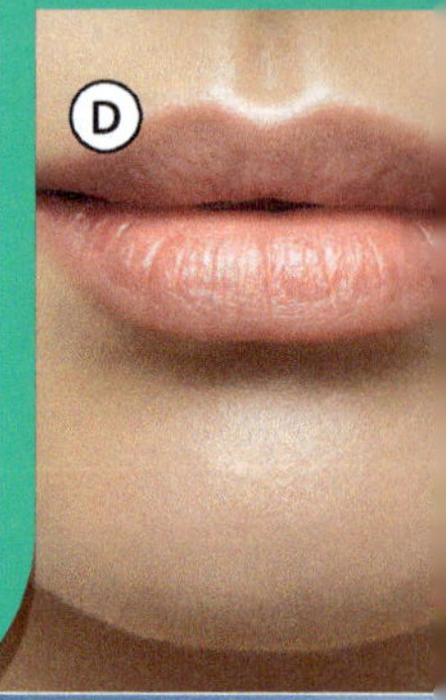

Vocabulary

1 **Name the things in photos A–I.**

2 **For each word in exercise 1, write the letter indicated.**

A	B	C	D	E	F	G	H	I
1st letter	1st letter	4th letter	3rd letter	3rd letter	6th letter	5th letter	4th letter	5th letter
A								

3 **Find three words for each group. If you need help, look at the unit.**

1. (Unit 7) jobs *artist, inventor, teacher*
2. (Unit 4) telling the time
3. (Unit 5) technology
4. (Unit 2) parts of the body
5. (Unit 8) transport
6. (Unit 3) shopping centre
7. (Unit 6) clothes and accessories
8. (Unit 3) food
9. (Unit 6) rooms and furniture

4 **Choose the correct option.**

1. I did my homework in five minutes. It was **easy/difficult**.
2. My friends and I don't go to the cinema. It's very **cheap/expensive**.
3. Don't come into the house with those shoes! They're **clean/dirty**.
4. We haven't got much time. Let's go by train – the bus is very **slow/fast**.
5. Can you help me carry this box of books? It's really **light/heavy**.
6. Do you like that book? Is it **boring/interesting**?

5 **Which verb goes with all of the words in each group?**

1. *do* your homework, sport
2. (…) basketball, video games, the guitar
3. (…) breakfast, lessons, dinner
4. (…) a taxi, photos, the train
5. (…) shopping, to bed, out on my bike

6 **Work in pairs. Complete the questions with verbs from exercise 5. Then ask and answer the questions for you.**

1. Where do you normally (…) shopping?
2. Can you (…) the guitar?
3. What time do you (…) breakfast?
4. Do you (…) a lot of photos with your friends?
5. How many times a week do you (…) video games?
6. What time do you (…) to bed at the weekend?

Reading

1 **Match 1–3 with a–c. They give advice from the Subskills in Units 1–8.**

1 Look at the photos and think what the text is about before you read it.
2 It's not important to understand every word the first time you read.
3 When you read for details, first look at the gaps and the words around them in the exercise.

a Then quickly find the information in the text.
b This can help you understand when you read.
c Just try to get a general idea.

2 **Work in pairs. Answer the questions (Subskill 1 in exercise 1).**

1 Describe what you can see in the photos.
2 What do you think happens at these festivals?

Exam tip
Remember to read the text quickly to get a general idea.

3 **Read the festivals guide quickly to check your answers to exercise 2 (Subskill 2).**

4 59 **Read and listen to the festivals guide. Copy and complete the table (Subskill 3).**

Name of the festival	La Tomatina	Songkran	Holi
What happens?	**1** People throw (…) .	**4** People have a (…) .	**8** People (…) , (…) and throw (…) .
Where?	**2** (…)	**5** (…)	**9** (…)
When?	**3** (…)	**6** (…)	March
Why?	No one knows	**7** (…)	**10** (…)

5 **Word work** **The words in bold in the festivals guide all appeared in the Word work exercises in Units 1–8. Can you remember what they mean?**

6 **Work in pairs. Take turns to say which festival you would most like to go to and why.**

A WORLD OF FESTIVAL FUN

Do you like going to festivals? Why not try one that is a bit different? Here are our favourites.

Our first is a tomato festival, but don't go if you're **hungry**: La Tomatina isn't about food or **diet**. It's a festival for people who want to go tomato-crazy! On the last Wednesday of August every year, there's a very big food fight in the village of Buñol, in Spain. It's strange, and no one knows why it started, but it's great **fun**. People come from all over the world just to throw tomatoes!

New Year is a big celebration all over the world, but the Songkran festival in Thailand is a New Year's party with a difference. People in Thailand celebrate New Year in April, and they want to clean everything for the start of the new year. So they have a water fight – for three days! It's one of the most popular festivals with visitors.

The Holi festival in India is one of the most beautiful festivals. At Holi, in the month of March, people celebrate the end of winter and the start of spring. Friends and relatives eat **together** and there's lots of dancing and singing. But the most **unusual** thing about Holi is that people throw water and paint: it's the festival of colours!

9 Look what you know!

Grammar

The questions in the white squares around the edge of the page help you remember the grammar you studied in the book.

First, answer the questions in square 1. Check your answers. Then do exercise 1.

Do the same with the other squares and exercises.

1 Complete the dialogue with the correct form of *be*.

A: Hi, **1** (…) you Scott?
B: No, I **2** (…) . Scott **3** (…) my brother. We **4** (…) twins.
A: You look the same! **5** (…) you similar in other ways?
B: No, we **6** (…) . I love basketball. I'm a Knicks fan, but Scott **7** (…) !

2 Choose the correct answers.

1 (…) a maths test today?
a You have got
b Have you got
c Have got you

2 Josh (…) his own room.
a haven't got **b** have got **c** hasn't got

3 (…) hair is long and curly.
a Megan **b** Megans' **c** Megan's

4 What kind of laptop (…) ?
a has your brother got
b your brother has got
c has got your brother

5 **A:** Has your school got a library?
B: Yes, it (…) .
a got **b** has **c** has got

3 Correct the incorrect sentences. Two sentences are correct.

1 There are some cold water in the fridge.
2 Is there a shopping centre near here?
3 There isn't a lot of restaurants in our town.
4 There is any fruit for dessert?
5 Can I have an apple, please?
6 There aren't some nice cafés near our school.

4 Rewrite the sentences in the affirmative (+) negative (-) or question (?) form.

1 I like sports. **(-)**
2 Your cousins don't live in the USA. **(?)**
3 Leticia doesn't watch TV every evening. **(+)**
4 Ömer has lunch at school. **(?)**
5 Azra doesn't study German. **(+)**
6 Do your parents speak English? **(-)**

5 Choose the correct option.

1 **Our/Ours** house is smaller than **their/theirs**.
2 **Can you/You can** speak French? No, I **can/can't**.
3 My bag is **heavier/more heavy** than **your/yours**.
4 I think maths is more **difficult/easy** than English.
5 My **younger/more young** brother can **swim/to swim** really well.
6 It's **more hotter/hotter** in Spain **that/than** in England.

6 Write sentences with the present continuous.

1 We / have / dinner / right now
2 My classmates / not / speak / English
3 What / you / do / at the moment ?
4 My sister / not / play a game; / she / study
5 Alice / sit / next to / Juan
6 Zeynep / chat / on the phone ?

8

1 Rewrite the sentence in the past simple: *We don't go by bus.*
2 How do we make a past simple negative?
3 Order the words: *you / last night / watch TV / did ?*

9

1 Choose the correct option: We use the superlative to compare **two/three or more** things.
2 Write the superlative form of *fast, busy, expensive, bad.*
3 Complete the sentence: *I think Italy is (…) beautiful country in the world.*

1

1 Complete with the verb *be*: *I (…), he (…), they (…)*.

2 What is the negative of these forms?

3 Order the words: *tired / are / you ?*

2

1 Choose the correct option: *He* ***have/has*** *got two brothers.*

2 Complete the question: *(…) you got any cousins?*

3 Correct or incorrect? *My parent's car is blue.*

3

1 Countable or uncountable? *water, potato, cheese, biscuit*

2 What is the difference between *some* and *any*?

3 Write the question. *Yes, there is. There's a lot of pizza.*

4

1 Make the sentence negative: *She likes football.*

2 Write the question: *I get up at 7:30.*

3 Complete the list: *me, you, him, (…), (…), (…).*

5

1 Choose the correct option: *I can't* ***draw/to draw***.

2 Correct the sentence: *Turkey is more big than England.*

3 Complete the list: *my – mine, your – yours, his – (…), (…) – (…), (…) – (…), (…) – (…).*

6

1 When do we use the present continuous?

2 Write the sentence: *It / not / rain / at the moment*

3 Order the words: *they / are / doing / what ?*

7

1 Rewrite the sentence in the past simple: *Is he famous?*

2 Complete the rule: We add (…) to regular verbs to make the past simple.

3 What is the past simple form of these verbs? *go, do, see, take*

7 Complete the text with the past simple form of the verbs in brackets.

Most people say that Wilbur and Orville Wright **1** (…) **(invent)** the plane. The brothers **2** (…) **(be)** from Ohio, in the USA. They **3** (…) **(want)** to be inventors from a young age, and they **4** (…) **(study)** birds to learn about flying.

It **5** (…) **(not be)** easy to build a plane. The brothers' first flight in 1903 only **6** (…) **(last)** 12 seconds. But they **7** (…) **(travel)** around the world and they **8** (…) **(continue)** to make planes. Today, we can all fly to different countries.

8 Rewrite the sentences. Write one sentence with a negative verb and one *Yes/No* question.

1 I visited my grandparents last Sunday.
I didn't visit my grandparents last Sunday. Did you visit your grandparents last Sunday?

2 I saw the match on TV.

3 We had chicken for dinner.

4 They went to the cinema last night.

5 I got up at half past six.

6 Leslie met her best friend on holiday.

9 Complete the questions. Then answer them for you.

1 Who is (…) **(famous)** person you know?

2 What is (…) **(big)** city in your country?

3 What is (…) **(dangerous)** way to travel?

4 What is (…) **(healthy)** sport?

5 Where is (…) **(good)** place to go on holiday?

6 What is (…) **(popular)** TV series at the moment?

Listening

1 Work in pairs. Think of three or more words or expressions for the following:

1 adjectives to describe a person
2 phrases to say the time
3 prepositions to describe the position of something
4 personal objects
5 types of transport

2 60 Listen to five short conversations. For each conversation, choose the best picture to answer the question.

1 Which girl is Layla?

2 What time does the festival start?

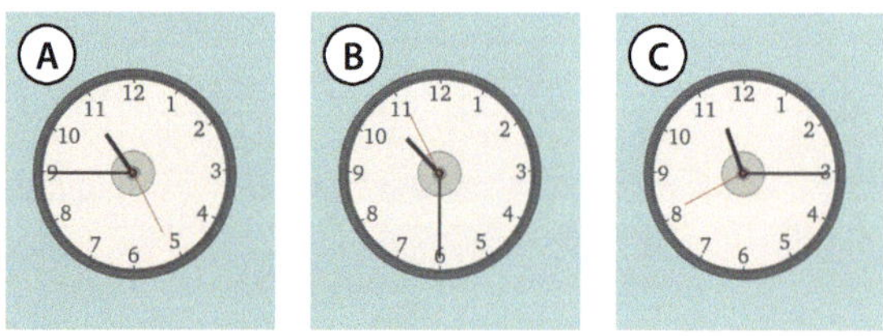

3 Where is the café?

4 What does the boy decide to buy for his mum?

5 How do they get home?

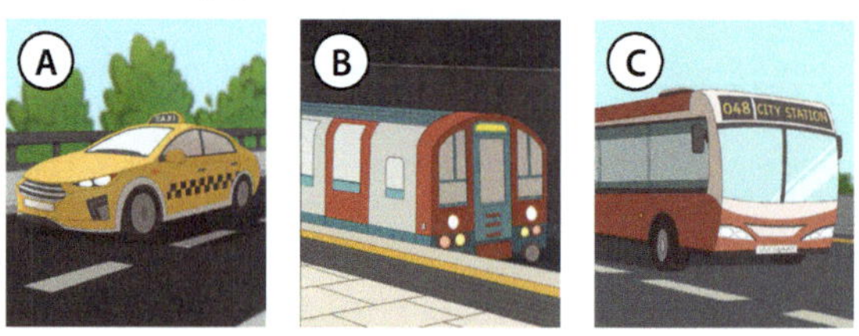

3 Work in pairs. Look at the photo and answer the questions.

1 What can you see?
2 Where do you think this is?
3 What do you think people do here?

4 61 Listen to a podcast about a winter festival. Choose the correct answers.

Exam tip

Don't worry if you don't answer all the questions the first time you listen. You hear the audio twice.

1 The Harbin festival is in …
  a the coldest place in the world.
  b a part of China.
  c Siberia.
2 They built the first ice sculptures …
  a in the 1960s.
  b thousands of years ago.
  c to celebrate the year 2000.
3 At the festival, visitors can …
  a do sports.
  b try to build the best sculpture.
  c enter a competition.
4 The festival …
  a starts in January.
  b continues for more than a month.
  c always finishes in March.
5 'Piroshki' is …
  a a type of food with meat or vegetables.
  b a typical potato dish.
  c the local tea.

5 Listen again and check your answers in exercise 4.

6 Work in pairs. Answer the questions.

1 What do you think is the most interesting thing about the festival?
2 Would you like to go there? Why/Why not?

Real-world speaking

1 Work in pairs. Look at the photos of two different festivals. Discuss the questions.

1 What type of festival is it?
2 Which festival would you prefer to visit? Why?

2 When do we use the Key phrases in the box? Copy and complete the table.

Buy your ticket on the bus. How can I get to (…) ? How much does it cost? How was your weekend? It's a great photo! It was great! Take the bus from the station. Who's this?

Talking about last weekend	
Asking for information	
Talking about a photo	
Buying a ticket	

3 62 **Listen and complete the dialogues.**

Conversation 1

How **1** (…) your weekend?

It was great. Jo and I went to the Lakefest BMX festival.

Who's **2** (…) on the bike?

It's Jo's cousin, Dani. He's really nice.

It's a **3** (…) photo.

Conversation 2

How can I **4** (…) to the balloon festival?

5 (…) the special bus from Temple Meads station.

How **6** (…) does it cost?

£1.20. **7** (…) your ticket on the bus.

OK, thanks.

4 Listen again and check. Who is speaking in each dialogue? Where are the people?

Exam tip

If you don't understand what to do, check with your teacher before you start.

5 Create your own dialogue for one of these situations. Follow the steps in the Skills boost.

A You're with a friend.
Ask about something they did recently.
Ask them to show you photos of the event and talk about them.

B You're at a tourist information office.
Ask for information about a place you want to visit.
Ask for information about how to get there.

SKILLS BOOST

THINK

1 Choose situation A or B.
2 Look at the phrases on this page, and Key phrases on the Real-world speaking pages. Choose at least six phrases to use in your dialogue.

PREPARE

Write your dialogue.

PRACTISE

Practise your dialogue. Try to remember it.

- First read the dialogue.
- Take turns saying your words from memory, while your partner reads and corrects.
- Practise saying the dialogue without reading.

PERFORM

Act out your dialogue for the class.

6 Peer review Listen to your classmates and answer the questions.

1 Which task did they choose?
2 Did they act out the dialogue from memory?
3 How many Key phrases did they use? Can you remember them?

Writing

1 Look at the writing sections in the book. Answer the questions.

1 In which unit did you write: an advert, a blog, an email, a story?

2 What other texts did you write?

2 Read texts A–C. What type of text is each one?

A New posts Archives

A special day! Posted 12th June

Winters are cold and dark in Sweden, so the Midsummer festival is a special day. It's usually on 24th June. People wear traditional clothes and dance. We have a picnic and eat typical food – fish with potatoes. Then in the evening, we pick flowers and sleep with them under our head. It's …

B **Louis** To: Jasper

Hi Jasper,

How are you? I'm busy because we've got exams soon, but I wanted to tell you about last weekend. I went to a great party on Saturday. It was a friend's birthday and he had a barbecue. (I'm sending you a photo!) Then on Sunday it was our local festival. I met …

C

THE DAY I MET A GOOD FRIEND

I remember the day I met Rosa. It was on my first day at school. I was worried before I arrived because I didn't know any of the other students. But then I sat next to Rosa. I was shy, but she started chatting to me. She also helped me during the lesson. Now she's one of my best friends.

3 Find these things in the texts in exercise 2 and answer the questions.

1 a capital letter for a country, month and day
When else do we use capital letters? (Unit 1)

2 two apostrophes
When do we use apostrophes? (Unit 2)

3 two examples of *and* and *but*
Which do we use to add information? (Unit 3)

4 an example of *so* and *because*
Which do we use to give a reason? Which do we use to give a result? (Unit 4, Unit 6)

5 an example of *also*
We use also to add another fact. What is its position in a sentence? (Unit 7)

6 an example of *before* or *after*
Before school started, I was worried. Which action is first? (Unit 8)

4 Choose one task and write your answer. Write 100 words. Follow the steps in the Skills boost.

A Write a blog about a festival in your country.

B Write an email to a friend. Tell him/her about your last weekend.

C Write a story about the day you met a friend. Describe your friend then and now.

Exam tip

Think of ideas and organise them into paragraphs before you start to write.

SKILLS BOOST

THINK

1 Make notes about what information to include.

2 Think about the verb tenses. Are you writing about the present or the past?

PREPARE

Organise your writing into three paragraphs.

WRITE

Write your blog, email or story.

CHECK

Read your text. Answer the questions.

1 Is the grammar correct?

2 Is the punctuation correct?

3 Do you use connecting words (*and*, *but*, *because*, etc.)?

5 Peer review Work in groups. Read your classmates' texts. Answer the questions.

1 Is the punctuation correct?

2 Does the writer use connecting words?

3 What did you like about the blog, email or story?

REVIEW GAME

Key phrases:

You start.
Whose turn is it?
It's your/my turn.
What's the question?

How to play the 'SNAKE CHALLENGE'

1 Form groups of three to five students.
2 Each student needs a different coin or marker. Put these on START.
3 Take turns to roll a dice, move forward and do what it says on the square.
4 The winner is the first to FINISH!

START

1 Count from 100 to 90 – backwards!

2 Name six rooms or things you can find in a house.

3 Give your classmates four instructions.

4 MISS A TURN

5 Spell the names of three countries.

6 Say four adjectives.

7 GO BACK THREE SQUARES

8 Compare two people in the class.

9 Name six shops.

10 Speak for one minute about your family.

11 Say what you had for lunch yesterday.

12 Talk about a typical day. Say what time you do things.

13 GO FORWARD TWO SQUARES

14 Name a sport you do and a sport you would love to do.

15 Work in pairs. Make plans to meet next weekend.

16 GO BACK TO START

17 Say two things you can do well and two things you can't do.

18 MISS A TURN

19 Describe what someone in your group is wearing.

20 You have one minute. How many forms of transport can you name?

21 Ask someone in your group a question about jobs.

FINISH

Grammar bootcamp

Starter unit

Subject pronouns and possessive adjectives

1 **Choose the correct option.**

1 That's Mrs. Green. **She/Her** is the new teacher.
2 Is that **you/your** mobile phone?
3 Alexa and Zadie are sisters. **They/Their** surname is Kent.
4 I go to a good school. **It/Its** isn't very big.
5 Jack and **he/his** friend are in the same class.
6 This isn't **we/our** classroom this year.

2 **Complete the email with subject pronouns and possessive adjectives.**

William To: Dan Subject: Hello!

Hi! **1** (…) name's William. **2** (…) 'm 11 years old. This is a photo of me and my family. **3** (…) live in Liverpool and that's **4** (…) house. My parents are teachers. **5** (…) names are Jayne and Oliver. **6** (…) teach at my school. My dad likes football – **7** (…) 's a Liverpool fan, like me. My sister is on the left. **8** (…) name's Ellen and **9** (…) 's a student. And that's my sister's dog. **10** (…) name is Coco. What about you? Where are **11** (…) from? What are **12** (…) hobbies?

a, an and plurals

3 **Complete the sentences with *a* or *an*.**

1 Have you got (…) email address?
2 I live in (…) small city in Scotland.
3 Ed Sheeran is (…) English singer.
4 The USA is (…) big country.
5 Is that (…) new computer?
6 I've got (…) orange pencil case.

4 **Write the plural of words 1–10.**

1 baby
2 box
3 diary
4 umbrella
5 notebook
6 party
7 phone
8 sandwich
9 toy
10 family

this, that, these, those

5 **Write sentences with *this, that, these* or *those*.**

this/these that/those

1 is my new mobile phone.
This is my new mobile phone.
2 Are your books over there?
3 aren't my keys. Where are my keys?
4 Is your umbrella? Can I borrow it?
5 are the notes for my project.
6 is an easy exercise!

Imperatives

6 **Write rules. Use the affirmative or negative imperative form of the verbs in the box.**

ask questions	be late	do your homework
eat or drink	listen	use your mobile phone

1 (…) to your classmates.

2 (…) in class.

3 (…) when you don't understand.

4 (…) for class.

5 (…) in the classroom.

6 (…) every evening.

Unit 1

be: affirmative

1 Reinforcement **Match the pronouns and the forms of the verb *be*.**

I am

it we you they

am are is

he she I

2 Reinforcement **Write the contracted forms of the verbs in exercise 1.**

I'm

3 Reinforcement **Choose the correct option.**

1 Amsterdam **is/are** the capital of the Netherlands.
2 I**'m/'re** from a small town in the USA.
3 Beijing and Shanghai **is/are** in China.
4 Australia **am/is** a big country.
5 My parents **is/are** Mexican.

4 Challenge **Complete the email with the correct form of *be*. Use contracted forms where possible.**

Andres To: Lucy Subject: Hello!

Hi Lucy!

My name **1** (…) Andres and I **2** (…) Colombian. My parents **3** (…) called Ayleen and Carlos, and my sister **4** (…) called Laura. We **5** (…) from Bogotá, the capital of Colombia. Bogotá **6** (…) a big city – the population is about seven million – and it **7** (…) a great place to live. People **8** (…) very happy here. Music and football **9** (…) popular – and yellow **10** (…) our favourite colour – it **11** (…) the colour of our national football team. **12** (…) you a fan of football? Let me know!

Andres

be: negative

5 Reinforcement **Complete the sentences with the negative form of *be*.**

1 Madrid is in Spain. It (…) in Mexico.
2 We're Chinese. We (…) Japanese.
3 Istanbul and Ankara are big Turkish cities. They (…) small.
4 I'm in class now. I (…) at home.
5 Rosalía (…) an actor. She's a singer.
6 You (…) from the USA. You're from the UK.

6 Challenge **Write sentences with the words in the table. Use contracted forms of *be*. How many sentences can you write?**

Mexico	is	from	not
are	I	He	We
am	They	Turkish	You

I'm from Mexico.

be: questions and short answers

7 Reinforcement **Write questions with *be*.**

1 You're from New Zealand.
Are you from New Zealand?
2 New York City is noisy.
3 We're in a different classroom today.
4 The parks are beautiful.
5 I'm late.
6 The capital city is very expensive.

8 Reinforcement **Choose the correct answers to the questions in exercise 7.**

1	a No, I'm not.	b No, it isn't.
2	a Yes, it is.	b Yes, they are.
3	a No, we not.	b No, we aren't.
4	a Yes, they're.	b Yes, they are.
5	a Yes, I'm.	b Yes, you are.
6	a Yes, it is.	b Yes, it's.

9 Challenge **Write questions with *be*.**

1 you / from Australia ?
2 Sydney / the capital city ?
3 your parks / big ?
4 it / hot in summer ?
5 we / the same age ?
6 you / a fan of rugby ?

10 Challenge **Complete the short answers to the questions in exercise 9.**

1 Yes, (…) .
2 No, (…) .
3 Yes, (…) .
4 Yes, (…) .
5 Yes, (…) .
6 No, (…) .

Unit 2

have got: affirmative and negative

1 Reinforcement **Rewrite the sentences with contracted forms.**

1 I have got brown hair.
I've got brown hair.
2 We have got three cousins.
3 Jane and Phil have not got any children.
4 I have not got short hair.
5 My uncle has got a beard.
6 Hannah has not got a sister.
7 You have got straight hair.
8 He has got blue eyes.
9 They have not got any nieces and nephews.

2 Challenge **Look at the photos and write sentences. Use pronouns and affirmative or negative contracted forms.**

1 Alex / brown eyes
He's got brown eyes.
2 I / short hair
3 Nina and I / long hair
4 I / curly hair
5 Nina / curly hair
6 Nina and I / straight hair
7 Nina and Alex / brown eyes

Possessive *'s*

3 Reinforcement **Write apostrophes in the correct position.**

1 My brothers name is Billy.
2 My grandparents car is very old.
3 My sisters names are Jane and Clara.
4 My music teacher is my mums best friend.
5 My friends phone number is 626 000 626.
6 This is my parents favourite restaurant.

4 Challenge **Write apostrophes in the correct position. Is the apostrophe for a contracted form (C) or for possession (P)?**

My dads got a brother and a sister, Phil and Louise. My uncle Phils tall and dark and hes got two daughters. My cousins names are Lily and Rose. My aunt Louise is a doctor and my aunts husbands an actor. His names Troy. Today is my aunts birthday and were all at her house for a party.

have got: questions and short answers

5 Reinforcement **Write questions for the questionnaire.**

Questionnaire:
Your family

1. you / any cousins ?
   Have you got any cousins?
2. you / any brothers or sisters ?
3. your mum / long hair ?
4. your grandparents / a car ?
5. your friend / blue eyes ?
6. your class / maths today ?
7. your classroom / a computer ?

6 Reinforcement **Match the answers in the box with the questions in exercise 5.**

No, I haven't.	No, they haven't.	No, we haven't.
Yes, he has.	~~Yes, I have.~~	Yes, it has.	Yes, she has.

1 Yes, I have.

7 Challenge **Write questions with *a*, *an* or *any*.**

1. you / bike ?
   Have you got a bike?
2. you / uncle ?
3. your friend / favourite singer ?
4. your mum or dad / Instagram account ?
5. your friend / brothers or sisters ?
6. you / twin ?

8 Challenge **Match the answers in the box with the questions in exercise 7.**

No, he's an only child.
No, I haven't, but I've got three aunts.
No, I haven't, but my cousins are twins.
Yes, she has.
My mum has, and she's got about 200 followers.
~~Yes, I have.~~

1 Yes, I have.

9 Challenge **Write answers for the questions in exercise 7 so they are true for you.**

Unit 3

Countable and uncountable

1 Reinforcement **Are nouns 1–8 countable (C) or uncountable (U)?**

1. bread
   U
2. potato
3. soup
4. sandwich
5. orange
6. cheese
7. meat
8. biscuit

2 Reinforcement **Write *a*/*an* before the countable nouns, and *some* before the uncountable nouns in exercise 1.**

1 some bread

3 Challenge **Complete the sentences with *a*/*an* or *some* and the words in the box.**

biscuit	oil	orange	pasta	sandwich

1. I've got (…) with cheese and tomato in it for my lunch.
2. We have (…) with tomato sauce for dinner on Sundays.
3. My mum puts some salt, vinegar and (…) on her salad.
4. I don't want an apple. I want (…) .
5. Can I have (…) with my coffee, please?

some, any, a lot of

4 Reinforcement **Choose the correct option.**

1. We haven't got **some/any** cheese.
2. I'd like **some/any** water, please.
3. Have we got **some/any** apples?
4. We need **some/any** chocolate to make this dessert.
5. I can't drink this coffee. It hasn't got **some/any** milk in it.
6. Have you got **some/any** biscuits? I'm hungry!
7. I usually have **some/any** fruit after lunch.

5 Challenge **Complete the dialogue with *a*, *an*, *some*, *any* or *a lot of*.**

Esme: Have we got **1** (…) drinks for the party?
Molly: We've got **2** (…) water – 20 bottles! But we haven't got **3** (…) fruit juice.
Esme: I can get **4** (…) fruit juice. I've got **5** (…) list of things to buy.
Molly: We've only got five pizzas. We need **6** (…) food for 40 people!
Esme: I can buy **7** (…) more.
Molly: And don't forget to buy **8** (…) orange cake for my birthday!

there is/ are

6 Reinforcement **Look at the picture. Complete the sentences with *'s*, *isn't*, *are* or *aren't*.**

1 There (…) a café.
2 There (…) a hairdresser's.
3 There (…) some people.
4 There (…) any restaurants.
5 There (…) a newsagent's.

7 Reinforcement **Complete the questions about the picture in exercise 6 with *Is there* or *Are there*.**

1 (…) a dog?
2 (…) any clothes shops?
3 (…) a cinema?
4 (…) any comics at the newsagent's?
5 (…) a shoe shop?

8 Reinforcement **Answer the questions in exercise 7.**

9 Challenge **Look at the picture in exercise 6. Write sentences with *There's*, *There isn't*, *There are* or *There aren't* and the words in the box. Use *some* and *any* when necessary.**

a chemist's a food stall a newsagent's bread at the baker's sports shops tables and chairs

10 Challenge **Write questions about the picture in exercise 6 with the words in the box. Then write short answers.**

a café a supermarket comics fruit people restaurants

Unit 4

Present simple: affirmative and negative

1 Reinforcement **Write the third person singular of the verbs.**

1 copy
2 do
3 drink
4 finish
5 get up
6 go
7 have
8 relax
9 study

2 Reinforcement **Complete the sentences with the present simple of the verbs in brackets.**

1 My mother *finishes* **(finish)** work at 6:00 pm.
2 My friend and I (…) **(do)** our homework together.
3 On Saturdays, I (…) **(get up)** at 10:00 am.
4 Nadeem (…) **(go)** to school by bus.
5 My dad (…) **(have)** lunch at home.
6 My sister (…) **(study)** French at university.
7 My brother (…) **(drink)** tea and I (…) **(have)** water.

3 Reinforcement **Change the sentences in exercise 2 from affirmative to negative.**

1 My mother doesn't finish work at 6:00 pm.

4 **Challenge** **Complete the sentences with the affirmative form of the verbs from exercise 1. There are two verbs you don't need.**

1 Adriana (…) at 7:00 am.
2 My parents (…) coffee for breakfast.
3 My cousin and I (…) at the same school.
4 I (…) school at 4:00 pm.
5 My sister (…) her homework in the afternoon.
6 Jonas (…) for an hour before he (…) to bed.

5 **Challenge** **Complete the text with the correct form of the verbs in brackets.**

A DAY IN THE LIFE OF A SWIMMER

I **1** (…) **(get up +)** at half past five. I **2** (…) **(eat -)** anything, but I **3** (…) **(drink +)** some water and then I **4** (…) **(go +)** to the sports centre. The training **5** (…) **(start -)** in the pool, it **6** (…) **(start +)** in the gym. Then I **7** (…) **(swim +)** for an hour. After that, I **8** (…) **(have +)** breakfast and then my school day **9** (…) **(start +)**.

School **10** (…) **(finish +)** at three o'clock, and at four I'm in the pool again. After dinner, I **11** (…) **(want +)** to relax, but first it's time for homework. I **12** (…) **(go -)** to bed late – usually at about ten.

6 **Challenge** **Rewrite the text in exercise 5 so it is about a swimmer called James.**

1 James gets up at half past five.

Present simple: *Yes/No* and *Wh-* questions

7 **Reinforcement** **Write *Yes/No* questions and short affirmative or negative answers.**

1 British people / play rugby ? **(+)**
Do British people play rugby? Yes, they do.
2 penguins / live in the Arctic ? **(-)**
3 Millie Bobby Brown / come from / the USA ? **(-)**
4 people from the Netherlands / speak Dutch ? **(+)**
5 Will Smith's son / sing rap music ? **(+)**
6 Naomi Osaka / play tennis ? **(+)**
7 25 + 32 / make 58 ? **(-)**

8 **Reinforcement** **Look at the colours and make *Wh-* questions with *do* or *does*. Then answer the questions.**

When	do/does	you	your friend
Where	go to school	How	have lunch

1 When does your friend have lunch? She has lunch at one o'clock.

9 **Challenge** **Order the words to make questions. Then answer them.**

1 do / what time / get up / at the weekend / you ?
2 have / for breakfast / what / do / your parents ?
3 like / your best friend / does / sport ?
4 go / how / you / do / to school ?
5 do / do / you / your / where / homework ?
6 in the morning / or in the evening / shower / do you have / a ?

love, like, don't like, hate + nouns and object pronouns

10 Reinforcement **Write sentences about the information in the table. Then rewrite the sentences with subject and object pronouns.**

	♥♥♥♥	♥♥♥♡	♥♡♡♡	♡♡♡♡
Gemma	pizza		bananas	tennis
Bobby and Flo	tennis	bananas	pizza	
I		pizza	tennis	bananas

Gemma loves pizza. She loves it.

11 Challenge **Write sentences with pronouns.**

1 Anna ♡♡♡♡ fish.
She hates it.
2 Simon ♥♥♥♡ rugby.
3 Ingrid and Pol ♥♡♡♡ Mrs Brown.
4 My sister and I ♥♥♥♥ Shawn Mendes.
5 Maria ♥♡♡♡ fruit and vegetables.
6 Our new cat ♥♥♥♡ my brother and me.

Unit 5

can and *can't*

1 Reinforcement **Complete the sentences with *can* or *can't* and the verbs in the box.**

catch climb cook repair sing walk

1 She (...) .

2 They (...) .

3 He (...) .

4 She (...) a mountain.

5 He (...) a ball.

6 I (...) my bike.

2 Reinforcement **Order the words to make questions.**

1 you / can / play the guitar ?
2 can / what languages / speak / you ?
3 your brother / drive / can ?
4 how fast / an elephant / can / run ?
5 dance / Tom and Evan / can ?

3 Reinforcement **Match questions 1–5 in exercise 2 with answers a–e. Complete the answers.**

a Yes, he (...) , but he hasn't got a car.
b No, they (...) . They're terrible!
c I (...) speak English and a little Spanish.
d No, I (...) , but I can play the piano.
e It (...) run 40 km an hour.

4 Challenge **Complete the advertisement with *can* or *can't* and the verbs in the box.**

answer do play run speak talk teach understand walk

Professor Reed

the robot that teaches maths and science

✓ answers science questions
✓ plays games
✓ walks and talks
✓ understands English

Meet Professor Reed. She's a robot and she **1** [...] you about science.

- She **2** [...] your homework for you, but she **3** [...] all your science and maths questions. And she **4** [...] games with you!
- She **5** [...] a lot of languages, but she **6** [...] English and she **7** [...] to you about the weather, famous people and food.
- She **8** [...] , but she **9** [...] and move her arms.

5 Challenge **Write questions with *can* for the answers. Start with the word in brackets.**

1 I can play the bass guitar. **(What)**
2 No, she can't. My dad speaks French, but not my mum. **(Can)**
3 I can cook Mexican food. **(What)**
4 Yes, it's E – X – P – E – N – S – I – V – E. **(Can)**
5 Not very fast. I'm not a good swimmer. **(How)**
6 Yes, I can. I sing all of Ariana Grande's songs. **(Can)**

Comparative adjectives

6 Reinforcement **Complete the text with comparative adjectives.**

The old computer is **1** (…) **(big)** than the new computer, but the screen is **2** (…) **(small)**. The old screen is **3** (…) **(bad)** for your eyes! The old computer is **4** (…) **(slow)** and **5** (…) **(heavy)**, and the keyboard is **6** (…) **(difficult)** to use, too.

The new computer is **7** (…) **(thin)**, and I think it's **8** (…) **(beautiful)**. It's probably also **9** (…) **(cheap)** than the old computer.

7 Challenge **Write ten sentences comparing the two phones.**

Phone **Reviews** News Reviews

	SAM	SAM 2
Date	2019	2020
Size	154x74x7 mm	156x75x6 mm
Weight	150 gr	140 gr
Price	€200	€250
Rating	★★★★	★★★★★

1 The SAM is older than the SAM 2.

Possessive pronouns

8 Reinforcement **Replace the underlined words with possessive pronouns.**

1. Our TV is bigger than <u>their TV</u>.
2. My brother uses my tablet and I use <u>his tablet</u>.
3. This isn't Ellen's laptop. <u>Her laptop</u> is in her bag.
4. Your phone is better than <u>my phone</u>.
5. My grandparents haven't got a laptop. They use <u>our laptop</u>.
6. Is this camera <u>your camera</u> or your dad's?

9 Challenge **Correct the incorrect pronouns. Two sentences are correct.**

1. I've got my books, but they haven't got their.
2. Your touchpad is easier to use than my.
3. Alex has got my phone and I've got his.
4. Whose charger is this? Is it your?
5. I sometimes use my sister's tablet. Her is better than mine.
6. My big camera is better than the camera on my phone.
7. This isn't your computer. It's our.

Unit 6

Present continuous: affirmative and negative

1 Reinforcement **Copy and complete the table with the *-ing* form of the verbs in the box.**

begin carry change copy get give introduce listen plan stop use wear work

+ *-ing*	e + *-ing*	double consonant + *-ing*
speaking	having	sitting

2 Reinforcement **Write sentences in the present continuous.**

1. Joe / listen to music *Joe is listening to music.*
2. We / work / in the garden
3. My grandmother / wear / her new trainers
4. My parents / plan / our new kitchen
5. I / go / school now
6. He / carry / an umbrella

3 Reinforcement **Change the sentences in exercise 2 from affirmative to negative.**

4 Challenge **Complete the dialogue with the affirmative (+) or negative (-) form of the verbs in the box.**

buy carry come stand use wear work

Lou: Hi. Where are you? I **1** (…) **(+)** at the ticket office, but I can't see you.

Billy: We **2** (…) **(-)** our tickets at the ticket office. We **3** (…) **(+)** one of the machines next to the Visitor Information Centre. I **4** (…) **(+)** my red jacket and Andi **5** (…) **(+)** a blue bag. But we've got a problem – the machine **6** (…) **(-)**!

Lou: OK – I can see you now. I **7** (…) **(+)** to meet you.

5 Challenge **What's happening now? Write sentences that are true for you.**

1 I / sit in the living room
I'm not sitting in the living room, I'm sitting in the classroom.
2 We / study / maths
3 My friend / sit / next to me
4 My parents / shop / at the moment
5 I / wear / jeans and trainers
6 Our teacher / correct exams
7 I / listen / to music

Present continuous: *Yes/No* questions and short answers

6 Reinforcement **Match questions 1–6 with answers a–f.**

1 Are you listening to music?
2 Are your parents working?
3 Is your brother running?
4 Are you and Anna watching a film?
5 Is your grandmother sleeping?
6 Am I asking questions?

a No, he isn't.
b Yes, she is.
c No, I'm not.
d Yes, you are.
e No, we aren't.
f Yes, they are.

7 Challenge **What are the people doing today? Write questions. Then answer them with the information in the calendar.**

Saturday 19

Mum	*Watch Ross / basketball*
Dad	*Shop*
Lily	*Violin lesson*
Ross	*Basketball match against the BB Lions*

1 Ross / play rugby ?
2 Mum / watch / Ross ?
3 Both parents / do the shopping ?
4 Mum and Ross / spend the morning together ?
5 Lily / have a piano lesson ?
6 Lily / spend the morning with her father ?

Present continuous: *Wh-* questions

8 Reinforcement **Complete the questions with the verbs in the box.**

~~cook~~	drink	go	listen to	look at	run	talk to

1

What *are you cooking*?

2

Where … ?

3

What … ?

4

What … ?

5

Who … ?

6

Why … ?

7

What … ?

9 **Challenge** **Write questions about the underlined information.**

1 I'm watching a film.
What are you watching?
2 I'm going to the shops.
3 Anne's talking to Claire.
4 We're eating pizza.
5 He's carrying ten books.
6 They're shopping now.
7 She's wearing a coat because it's cold.

Unit 7

Past simple of *be*: affirmative and negative

1 **Reinforcement** **Choose the correct option.**

1 Thomas Edison **wasn't/weren't** an astronaut. He **was/were** an inventor.
2 We **was/were** at home on Saturday. We **wasn't/weren't** at school.
3 My grandmother **was/were** a doctor. She **wasn't/weren't** a teacher.
4 Picasso and Dalí **wasn't/weren't** actors. They **was/were** artists.
5 I **wasn't/weren't** born in November. I **was/were** born in December.

2 **Challenge** **Complete the text with *was(n't)* or *were(n't)*.**

Famous people who weren't famous in their lifetime

There are a lot of artists, writers and musicians who are famous now, but who **1** (…) famous when they **2** (…) alive. Take Johann Sebastian Bach, for example. Most people today know that he **3** (…) a great German composer, but he **4** (…) famous in his lifetime.

Emily Dickinson is a well-known American poet now, but her poems **5** (…) popular when she was alive.

And then there are the two Dutch artists, Johannes Vermeer and Vincent Van Gogh. Vermeer **6** (…) born in 1632, but he **7** (…) famous until the 19th century. And Van Gogh only sold one painting, and he **8** (…) a poor man when he died.

Past simple of *be*: *Yes/No* questions and short answers

3 **Reinforcement** **Write questions. Then write affirmative or negative short answers.**

1 you / at school yesterday ? **(+)**
Were you at school yesterday? Yes, I was.
2 your friends / at home on Saturday ? **(-)**
3 it / cold yesterday ? **(-)**
4 your teacher / at school at eight o'clock ? **(+)**
5 you and your classmates / in the same classroom last year ? **(+)**
6 you / late this morning ? **(-)**

4 **Challenge** **Order the words to make questions.**

1 Ernest Shackleton / was / English ?
2 were / famous in Roman times / artists ?
3 were / on Instagram / you / in 2015 ?
4 was / a Mexican artist / Frida Kahlo ?
5 you and your friends / were / fans of The Beatles ?

5 **Challenge** **Complete the short answers. Then match the answers with the questions in exercise 4.**

a No, I (…) .
b Yes, she (…) .
c No, we (…) !
d Yes, they (…) .
e No, he (…) . He (…) Irish.

Past simple of *be*: *Wh-* questions

6 **Reinforcement** **Write *was* or *were* in the correct position. Then answer the questions so they were true for you in 2019.**

1 How old you?
2 What the name of your school?
3 Who your favourite singer?
4 What your favourite TV programmes?
5 Where your teacher from?
6 Who your friends?

7 **Challenge** **Write questions about the underlined information. Then answer the questions so they are true for you.**

1 I was born in 2010.
2 My first English teacher was Mr James.
3 Our last holiday was in March.
4 My first heroes were sports stars.
5 My favourite subject last year was history.
6 My friends and I were in the park on Saturday.

Past simple of regular verbs: affirmative

8 **Reinforcement** **Write sentences about João's day last Saturday.**

1 he / chat / online
2 he / walk / to a friend's house
3 they / play / video games
4 he / return / home
5 he / study / maths
6 he / watch / a film

9 **Challenge** **Complete the text with the past simple form of the verbs in the box.**

call	change	receive	start
travel	try	want	work

When he was 16, Alex Lee **1** (…) in a local shop in Texas. One day, a girl took a photo of him and posted it on social media. That photo **2** (…) Alex's life. The same day, people shared the photo 30,000 times, and Alex **3** (…) 10,000 messages on his phone. Soon, people **4** (…) to visit the shop because they **5** (…) to take a selfie with Alex. Then a famous TV personality, Ellen Degeneres, **6** (…) him and he **7** (…) to California to appear on her show. After that, he **8** (…) to live a normal life, but it was impossible. Now he's a social media star!

Past simple of irregular verbs: affirmative

10 **Reinforcement** **Write sentences with the past simple.**

Last Saturday, …

1 I / get up / at eight
2 I / have / breakfast
3 I / do / my homework
4 I / meet / my friend
5 We / go / to the cinema
6 We / see / a sci-fi film

11 **Challenge** **Rewrite the text with the verbs in the past simple.**

Charlotte D'Alessio becomes an Instagram star at the age of 16. She goes to a music festival with her friends. There, she and her friends wear different clothes. They take photos to post on social media. A famous photographer sees her photos and a newspaper writes a story about her. Soon after that, she leaves school. She begins to work as a model and she meets famous people, but she does lessons online at the same time.

Unit 8

Past simple: negative

1 **Reinforcement** **Write the infinitive of the verbs in the box.**

drank	had	met	saw	went

2 **Reinforcement** **Look at the pictures. Then correct the sentences about Cem's day.**

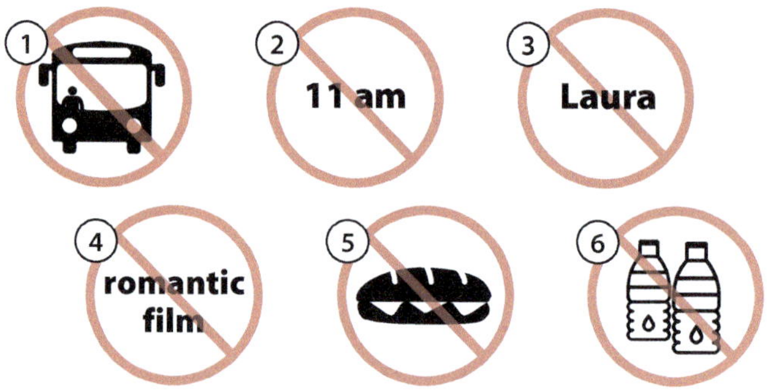

1 Cem *didn't go by bus*. He went by train.
2 Cem (…) . He went out in the afternoon.
3 He (…) . He met Mehmet.
4 They (…) . They saw an action film.
5 Cem (…) . He had a pizza.
6 They (…) . They drank cola.

3 **Challenge** **Read about Jack's dream. Then make the verbs negative.**

In my dream, I got up at seven because it was a school day. I had breakfast with my parents and I went to school by bike. My journey took 45 minutes. In the afternoon, I met my friend Rina. We went shopping and Rina bought a new pair of shoes. I went home by bus and I did my homework. I cooked dinner with my brother and I practised the clarinet. I went to bed at half past nine because I had school the next day.

But it was only a dream! In reality, yesterday was Saturday.

I didn't get up …

Past simple: questions and short answers

4 **Reinforcement** **Answer the questions.**

1 Did you go to school yesterday? **(-)**
No, I didn't.
2 Did your parents drive to work yesterday? **(+)**
3 Did you come to school by bus? **(-)**
4 Did you see an ambulance on your journey to school? **(+)**
5 Did you and your family go on holiday last year? **(-)**
6 Did your mother travel by metro last weekend? **(+)**
7 Did your best friend buy a travelcard last month? **(+)**

5 **Reinforcement** **Order the words to make questions. Then answer them so they are true for you.**

1 to a shopping centre / last go / when / you / did ?
2 go / you / did / where ?
3 go with / who / you / did ?
4 to the shops / how / you / go / did ?
5 buy / did / what / you ?
6 stay / how long / there / did / you ?

6 **Challenge** **Complete the dialogue.**

What **1** (…) last weekend?
I went to Guadalajara.
2 (…) ?
Because I wanted to watch a basketball match.
3 (…) ?
No, we went by coach.
4 (…) ?
About six hours.
5 (…) ?
No, we stayed there that night.
6 (…) ?
We stayed in a small hotel.
7 (…) ?
No, we lost 3–2.

Superlative adjectives

7 **Reinforcement** **Write the superlative forms of the adjectives in the box.**

bad beautiful big cheap fast good noisy popular

8 **Reinforcement** **Complete the sentences with the superlative form of the adjectives in exercise 7.**

1 (…) way to travel is on foot – it doesn't cost anything.
2 New York City has got (…) number of stations: 468!
3 If you haven't got much time, the plane is (…) form of transport. But it's also (…) for the environment.
4 We went on a tour of France. It's (…) country in the world, we took some amazing photos!
5 The helicopter is (…) form of transport. People usually wear headphones.
6 (…) way to travel in Tokyo is to take the underground. It's cheap, quick and comfortable.
7 In Amsterdam, bicycles are (…) way to travel, there are a lot of them in the streets.

9 **Challenge** **Complete the text with the superlative form of the adjectives in exercise 7.**

Madrid's top parks

Busy Madrid is also Spain's **1** (…) city, so if you need to relax somewhere quiet, the capital also has some great parks. Here are three of our favourites.

With thousands of visitors every day, the Retiro is Madrid's **2** (…) park in the city centre. It's also one of **3** (…) places to relax. The lake in the park is one of **4** (…) places in the city and a great place to take a selfie.

If you haven't got much money, one of **5** (…) ways to spend an afternoon is to go for a walk by the river at Madrid Río. **6** (…) way to get there from the city centre is by bus (ten minutes). But Sunday morning is **7** (…) time to go because it's very crowded.

With more than 1,500 hectares, the Casa de Campo is Madrid's **8** (…) park. The best way to go there is by cable car!

Pronunciation

Unit 1

Word stress

1 63 **Listen and repeat the countries in the table. Notice the word stress.**

Oo	oO	Ooo	oooO	oOoo
Russia	Brazil	Mexico	the USA	Australia

2 64 **Listen to countries 1–5. Add them to the correct column in exercise 1.**

1 India
2 Turkey
3 China
4 the Netherlands
5 Japan

3 **Listen again to the countries in exercises 1 and 2 and repeat.**

Unit 2

/ə/

The /ə/ sound is the most common sound in English. It's always in an unstressed syllable.

1 65 **Listen to the words and find the stressed syllable.**

mother father brother sister daughter

2 **Listen again. What is the pronunciation of the *-er* ending?**

3 **Repeat the words in exercise 1.**

4 **Find the stressed syllable in the words. Where is the /ə/ sound?**

America Australia Brazil China Canada
Italy India Japan Russia South Africa

5 66 **Listen and check. Then listen and repeat.**

Unit 3

Silent letters

1 67 **Look at the words. They all have silent letters (in red). Listen and repeat.**

bread chocolate juice

2 68 **Which letters are silent in these words? Listen and check.**

biscuit sandwich

3 69 **Work in pairs. Practise pronouncing these words. Then listen and check.**

beard beautiful daughter grandmother
interesting modern overweight straight

Unit 4

Pronouncing *-es* /ɪz/

We often pronounce -*es* in third person singular verbs /ɪz/, but we don't pronounce /ɪz/ when the verb ends in *o*, e.g. *goes*, *does*.

1 70 **Listen. Which verbs end in /ɪz/ after *he*/*she*/*it*?**

eats finishes gets goes relaxes
speaks starts studies watches

2 **Listen again and repeat.**

3 **Work in pairs. Practise saying the sentences. Pay attention to the /ɪz/ sound.**

1 My school day finishes at half past three.
2 My brother relaxes after school.
3 My cousin studies English at university.
4 My sister watches TV in her room.

Unit 5

Spelling the sound /iː/

Different groups of letters can make the /iː/ sound.

1 71 **Listen and underline the /iː/ sound.**

1 keyboard
2 screen
3 cheap
4 piece
5 police
6 people
7 niece
8 complete

2 **How can you spell the /iː/ sound?**

3 **Listen again and repeat the words in exercise 1.**

4 **Work in pairs. Practise saying the sentences. Focus on the /iː/ sound in the letters in bold.**

1 This k**ey**board isn't **ea**sy to k**ee**p cl**ea**n.
2 Can I have a p**ie**ce of ch**ee**se, pl**ea**se?
3 Some p**eo**ple can't r**ea**d the words on this scr**ee**n.
4 I n**ee**d to buy some ch**ea**p sp**ea**kers next w**ee**k.
5 My n**ie**ce r**ea**ds before she goes to sl**ee**p.

Unit 6

/e/ and /ɜː/

1 72 **Listen to the two sounds. Which sound is short? Which sound is long?**

1 /e/ 2 /ɜː/

2 73 **Copy and complete the table. Listen and write the words in the correct column.**

~~bed~~ end friend furniture girl head
her learn next test word work

/e/	/ɜː/
bed	

3 **Listen again and repeat the words in exercise 2.**

4 **Read the story. Do the words in bold have the sound /e/ or /ɜː/?**

Ellen studies English with **her friend Kirk**. They **work** hard and try to **learn** new **words**. One day, **Ellen** doesn't go to school because her **head hurts**. The **next** day, they have a **test**. **Ellen** is **nervous**, but she **gets ten** out of **ten**!

5 **Work in pairs. Take turns to read the story. Pay attention to the sounds /e/ and /ɜː/.**

Unit 7

was: weak and strong form

1 74 **Listen and repeat the two different ways we pronounce *was*. Then complete the rules.**

weak form /ə/	*He **was** an astronaut.*	***Was** he famous?*
strong form /ɒ/	*She **wasn't** a celebrity.*	*Yes, she **was**.*

1 For affirmative sentences and questions, we say
a /ə/ **b** /ɒ/
2 For negative sentences and short answers, we say
a /ə/ **b** /ɒ/

2 **Is *was* pronounced /ɒ/ or /ə/?**

A: Was Lucy in class?
B: Yes, she was. But she wasn't very happy.
A: Why not?
B: It was her birthday, but there was a maths exam!

3 **Practise reading the dialogue with a friend.**

Unit 8

Contracted forms

Contracted forms are when we join two words together. We omit a letter and use an apostrophe, e.g. *didn't* is the contracted form of *did not*.
*I **didn't** (did not) go to the cinema last weekend.*

1 **Write the contracted forms.**

1 was not
2 is not
3 did not
4 have not
5 were not
6 does not
7 has not
8 are not

2 75 **Listen to eight sentences. Write the number of words you hear in each one. (A contracted form is one word.)**

3 **Listen again and write the sentences in exercise 2.**

4 **Work in pairs. Practise saying the sentences. Pay attention to the contracted forms.**

Project planner

Unit 1 Graphic organiser

How are countries different?

- life in some countries
  - the Netherlands
  - New Zealand
- countries and nationalities
  - Brazil, Spain, Dutch, …
- teen life
  - education
  - food
  - free time
- adjectives
  - safe
  - crowded
  - modern

How to make a poster

- **Prepare** all the information first.
- **Get all the materials** you need (card, scissors, pens, glue, …).
- **Plan the space** before you start.
- **Put things in position** before you glue them.
- **Stand back** and look at your work from a distance.

Unit 2 Graphic organiser

What is a family?

- family members
  - uncle, cousin, niece, grandfather, …
- different types of family
  - advantages and disadvantages of big and small families
- different families
  - famous families, e.g. the Smiths
  - large families, e.g. the Putmans
- describing people
  - young
  - parts of the body
    - head, leg
  - hair
    - straight

How to give a presentation to other students

- **Practise** before you speak.
- Try to **remember the information**.
- **Don't read**. Try to speak from memory.
- **Look at the other students** while you speak.
- **Point at the pictures** to help other students follow your description.

Unit 3 Graphic organiser

- **What's the ideal meal?**
  - thinking about food
    - food from different countries
    - Meatless Mondays
  - food and drink
    - biscuit, sandwich, juice, …
  - places to eat and go shopping
    - baker's, supermarket, …
    - Hong Kong's unusual cafés
  - ordering food
    - prices: $2, £4.95, 'How much is that?'
    - 'Can I have some bread, please?'

How to prepare before you make a final copy

- Write notes and **organise your ideas**.
- Look at your paper and **plan how to use the space**.
- Think about **different styles of writing** for different parts.
- Think about using **photos or drawings** to make your presentation more attractive.

Unit 4 Graphic organiser

- **Why is it a good idea to organise your time?**
  - the time
    - quarter past two, twenty-five to ten
    - 'What time is it … ?'
    - 'What time do you … ?'
  - daily routine
    - do homework, have lunch, get up, …
  - organising a busy day
    - life in a K-pop academy
    - using mobile phone apps to help organise your life
    - advantages and disadvantages of a busy life
  - free-time activities
    - go out on my bike
    - meet friends
    - play video games
  - making plans
    - 'Sorry, I'm busy.'
    - 'Are you free on … ?'

How to create visual interest with photos

- Choose **different types of photos**, e.g. an object, a person, an activity.
- Use **bright colours**, e.g. red, blue or use **black and white**.
- Have **one main element** in the photo, and other small things.
- Include **things that aren't typical**.
- Choose an **unusual angle** for your photo, e.g. show hands or feet only.

Unit 5 Graphic organiser

- **Does technology make the world better? How?**
  - technology vocabulary
    - keyboard, tablet, screen, …
  - talk about abilities
    - send a text message
    - repair your bike
  - new technology
    - glasses for people who can't hear
    - 3D printers
  - comparing things
    - easier
    - more expensive
    - faster
  - amazing robots
    - prepare drinks, cook a meal, clean the kitchen, give information, …

How to make a digital presentation

- Use a **clear font** and make letters big.
- Include big, **attractive photos**.
- Have only **short texts** on the slides.
- **Prepare what to say** when you show each slide.
- **Print a copy** of the presentation.

Unit 6 Graphic organiser

- **What is art?**
  - Escape rooms: a real-life adventure game
    - A monster is waiting for you.
    - 221b Baker Street
  - the upside-down house
    - rooms and furniture: living room, bedroom, …
    - prepositions: on, between, under, …
  - asking for information
    - 'How can I get there?'
    - 'What time is it open?'
  - clothes
    - skirt, shirt, hat, …
  - artists at work
    - Street Style Surgery: art on T-shirts
    - Elisabeth Anisimow: living art

How to record an audio guide

- Decide what each person says.
- **Practise** first.
- Use a laptop or your phone.
- Choose a **quiet place** to make the recording.
- Remember to **speak slowly and clearly**.
- Do **two or more recordings**. Decide which is the best.

Unit 7 Graphic organiser

How to make a comic

- **Plan** your work before you start.
- **Draw the right number of boxes** and note the information for each one.
- Decide the **best picture** for each box.
- Start with an **attractive title** box.
- **Write clearly** – capital letters are easier to read.
- **Stand back** to look critically at your work.

Unit 8 Graphic organiser

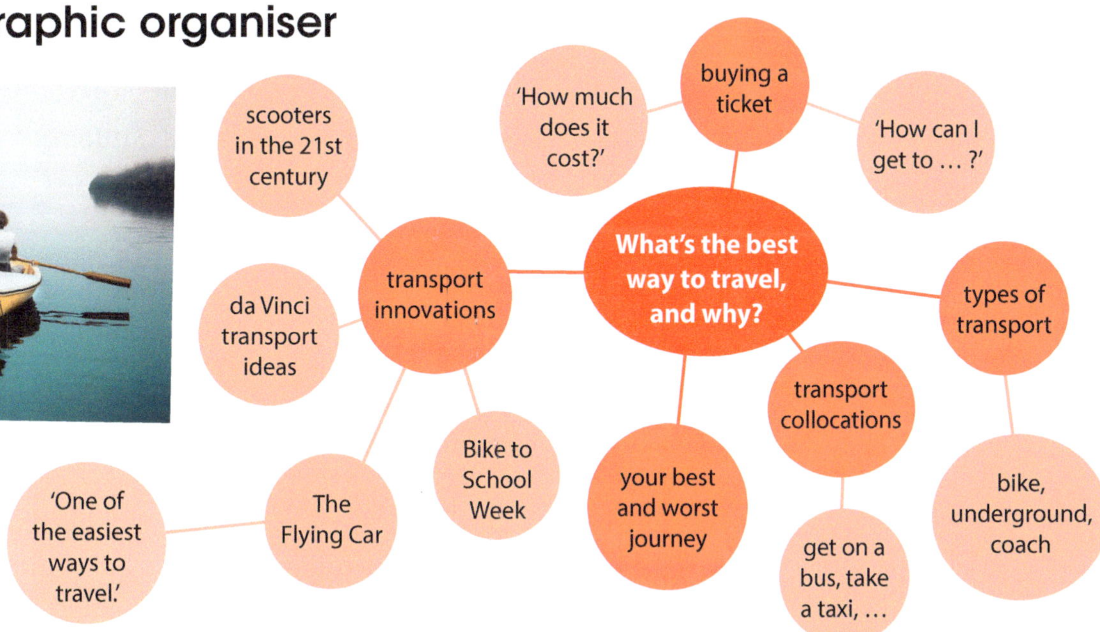

How to present the results of a survey

- **Count** the number of answers to each question.
- Use the number or **make a percentage**.
- Choose the **best way to present** the results, e.g. **a pie chart**, **a graph**.
- Draw the **visuals** by hand or use your computer to present the results.
- Ask: **What do the results tell us?**
- Write a **conclusion**.

Irregular verbs

Infinitive	Past simple	Past participle
be /biː/	**was/were** /wɒz/ /wɜː(r)/	**been** /biːn/
become /bɪˈkʌm/	**became** /bɪˈkeɪm/	**become** /bɪˈkʌm/
begin /bɪˈgɪn/	**began** /bɪˈgæn/	**begun** /bɪˈgʌn/
break /breɪk/	**broke** /brəʊk/	**broken** /ˈbrəʊkən/
bring /brɪŋ/	**brought** /brɔːt/	**brought** /brɔːt/
build /bɪld/	**built** /bɪlt/	**built** /bɪlt/
buy /baɪ/	**bought** /bɔːt/	**bought** /bɔːt/
catch /kætʃ/	**caught** /kɔːt/	**caught** /kɔːt/
choose /tʃuːz/	**chose** /tʃəʊz/	**chosen** /ˈtʃəʊz(ə)n/
come /kʌm/	**came** /keɪm/	**come** /kʌm/
cut /kʌt/	**cut** /kʌt/	**cut** /kʌt/
do /duː/	**did** /dɪd/	**done** /dʌn/
drink /drɪŋk/	**drank** /dræŋk/	**drunk** /drʌŋk/
drive /draɪv/	**drove** /drəʊv/	**driven** /ˈdrɪv(ə)n/
eat /iːt/	**ate** /eɪt/	**eaten** /ˈiːt(ə)n/
fall /fɔːl/	**fell** /fel/	**fallen** /ˈfɔːlən/
feed /fiːd/	**fed** /fed/	**fed** /fed/
feel /fiːl/	**felt** /felt/	**felt** /felt/
find /faɪnd/	**found** /faʊnd/	**found** /faʊnd/
fly /flaɪ/	**flew** /fluː/	**flown** /fləʊn/
forget /fə(r)ˈget/	**forgot** /fə(r)ˈgɒt/	**forgotten** /fə(r)ˈgɒt(ə)n/
get /get/	**got** /gɒt/	**got** /gɒt/
give /gɪv/	**gave** /geɪv/	**given** /ˈgɪv(ə)n/
go /gəʊ/	**went** /went/	**gone** /gɒn/
grow /grəʊ/	**grew** /gruː/	**grown** /grəʊn/
hang /hæŋ/	**hung** /hʌŋ/	**hung** /hʌŋ/
have /hæv/	**had** /hæd/	**had** /hæd/
hear /hɪə(r)/	**heard** /hɜː(r)d/	**heard** /hɜː(r)d/
hit /hɪt/	**hit** /hɪt/	**hit** /hɪt/
keep /kiːp/	**kept** /kept/	**kept** /kept/
know /nəʊ/	**knew** /njuː/	**known** /nəʊn/

Infinitive	Past simple	Past participle
lay /leɪ/	**laid** /leɪd/	**laid** /leɪd/
learn /lɜː(r)n/	**learnt/learned** /lɜː(r)nt/ /lɜː(r)nd/	**learnt/learned** /lɜː(r)nt/ /lɜː(r)nd/
leave /liːv/	**left** /left/	**left** /left/
let /let/	**let** /let/	**let** /let/
lose /luːz/	**lost** /lɒst/	**lost** /lɒst/
make /meɪk/	**made** /meɪd/	**made** /meɪd/
meet /miːt/	**met** /met/	**met** /met/
pay /peɪ/	**paid** /peɪd/	**paid** /peɪd/
put /pʊt/	**put** /pʊt/	**put** /pʊt/
read /riːd/	**read** /red/	**read** /red/
ride /raɪd/	**rode** /rəʊd/	**ridden** /ˈrɪd(ə)n/
ring /rɪŋ/	**rang** /ræŋ/	**rung** /rʌŋ/
run /rʌn/	**ran** /ræn/	**run** /rʌn/
say /seɪ/	**said** /sed/	**said** /sed/
see /siː/	**saw** /sɔː/	**seen** /siːn/
sell /sel/	**sold** /səʊld/	**sold** /səʊld/
send /send/	**sent** /sent/	**sent** /sent/
shine /ʃaɪn/	**shone** /ʃɒn/	**shone** /ʃɒn/
sing /sɪŋ/	**sang** /sæŋ/	**sung** /sʌŋ/
sit /sɪt/	**sat** /sæt/	**sat** /sæt/
sleep /sliːp/	**slept** /slept/	**slept** /slept/
speak /spiːk/	**spoke** /spəʊk/	**spoken** /ˈspəʊkən/
spend /spend/	**spent** /spent/	**spent** /spent/
sweep /swiːp/	**swept** /swept/	**swept** /swept/
swim /swɪm/	**swam** /swæm/	**swum** /swʌm/
take /teɪk/	**took** /tʊk/	**taken** /ˈteɪkən/
teach /tiːtʃ/	**taught** /tɔːt/	**taught** /tɔːt/
tell /tel/	**told** /təʊld/	**told** /təʊld/
think /θɪŋk/	**thought** /θɔːt/	**thought** /θɔːt/
throw /θrəʊ/	**threw** /θruː/	**thrown** /θrəʊn/
understand /ˌʌndə(r)ˈstænd/	**understood** /ˌʌndə(r)ˈstʊd/	**understood** /ˌʌndə(r)ˈstʊd/
wake /weɪk/	**woke** /wəʊk/	**woken** /ˈwəʊkən/
win /wɪn/	**won** /wʌn/	**won** /wʌn/
write /raɪt/	**wrote** /rəʊt/	**written** /ˈrɪt(ə)n/

Macmillan Education Limited
4 Crinan Street
London N1 9XW

Companies and representatives throughout the world

Influence Student's Book Intro ISBN 978-1-380-03271-3
Influence Student's Book Intro with Student's App ISBN 978-1-380-05416-6

First published 2021

Original design by Designers Collective Ltd and emc design ltd
Page make-up by emc design ltd
Illustrated by Camille Ferrari (Lemonade Illustration Agency) pp6, 100, 122(l); Janos Jantner (Beehive Illustration) pp60–61; Tamara Joubert (Beehive Illustration) pp48, 67; Carl Morris (Beehive Illustration) pp7, 95, 112(1,2,4,5); Martin Sanders (Beehive Illustration) p112(3); Nuno Viera (Beehive Illustration) pp8, 9(t), 40, 87, 103, 117, 120, 122(r), 124
Cover design by Designers Educational
Cover photograph by Getty Images
Picture research by Penelope Bowden, Proudfoot Pictures

Authors' acknowledgements
Gill would like to thank her friends from International House, Barcelona.
Kate would like to thank all her colleagues and friends at International House, Madrid.

The publishers would like to thank Ángeles Jimenez Fernández, I.E.S. El Car, San Cugat del Vallés, Barcelona; Andikona Loizate, Col.legi Pompeu Fabra-Guimera, Salt, Girona; Verónica Martín Martínez, Barcelona, Ana Mar Caballero, Col.legi María Auxiliadora, Zaragoza; Beatriz Sayalero Martín, I.E.S. Gran Capitán, Madrid; Begoña García Pérez, I.E.S. Gabriel García Márquez, Leganés, Madrid; María Purificación Pascual Mateos, Colegio Fundación Santamarca, Madrid; Rosa Victor Raurich, Col. legi Les Heures, Lleida; Núria Vallet Muntada, Institut Viladecavalls, Viladecavalls, Barcelona; Esther Valbuena Ibáñez, C.E.I.P. Ntra. Sra. Begoña, Bilbao, Vizcaya; Cristina Cano, I.E.S. Laguna de Joatzel, Getafe, Madrid; Marcia Loma-Osorio, I.E.S. Laguna de Joatzel, Getafe, Madrid; Mª Rosaura Marcos González, I.E.S. Luis García Berlanga, Coslada, Madrid; Sandra Valera, Colegio Santa Rita, Madrid; Maria Luisa Robledo, Colegio Salesianos San Juan Bautista, Madrid; Llorenç Rosselló Verger Col.legi Sant Jossep Obrer, Palma de Mallorca, Baleares; Vicent Pérez Zaragoza, I.E.S. Beatriz Fajardo de Mendoza, Benidorm, Alicante; Osvaldo Arroyo Caballero, México.

The authors and publishers would like to thank the following for permission to reproduce their photographs:
Alamy Images pp17(lc), 37(12), 75(5), 77(1), 125(b), Contributor: Everett Collection, Inc. p79(tm), Granger Historical Picture Archive p125(tmr), Loop Images Ltd p75(mr), photonic 20 p1169(diary), Paul Quayle pp11(9), 72(a, centre), 73(b), 73(c), 73(d), 132(b), Alex Segre pp73(e), 127, James Thew p79(tr); **Anisimow Art** p76; **Corbis** p17(ball); **Gary Roberts Photography** pp11, 29; **Getty Images** pp17(sheep), 23(tl), 36, 37(background), 37(6), 37(11), 104(background), 16(box), aaaaimages p51(br), Tobias Ackeborn pp96,97(a), AFP Contributor/Contributor p54, ALAMA p65(h), aldomurillo p117, Igor Alecsander p44(2), ALLEKO pp11(4), 44(4), Steve Allen p17(tr), Troy Aossey p83(2), Arctic-Images pp24,25(background), Anadolu Agency/Contributor p63(br), avid_creative p80(Eric), Baks p115(ball), Santiago Bañón p118(Alex), Barcin p37(10), Thomas Barwick pp41(5), 91(tc), 114(c), Best Content Production Group p75(lasers), Bettmann/Contributor pp11(1), 85(ml), 87(bl), bildfokus p114(a), Paul Biris pp82, 83(background), blackred pp94, 95, Bloom Productions p18, Massimo Borchi/Atlantide Phototravel p41(3), FREDERIC J. BROWN/Staff pp65(1), 132(mr), brusinski p24(Williams), Adrian Burke p37(4), Cris Cantón p12(croquetas), Capuski p65(3), carloscastilla p50(6), carlosgaw p13(beans), Angelo Cavalli p108(i), Cavan Images p99(b), Caziopeia p116(sandwich), CBCK-Christine p36(a), Kae Ch/EyeEm p65(e), ChamilleWhite p59(1), Poras Chaudhary pp109(br), 131(b), Chrupka p12(patatas), Matthias Clamer p83(1), Chris Clor p75(t), Compassionate Eye Foundation/Steven Errico p15(bmc), ConstantinosZ p37(8), Maribel Coppen-Gardner/EyeEm p35(lt), Iulia Cozlenco 14(b), Creative Crop p68(tl), Cultura RF pp108(e), 115(girl), DAJ p20(lm), DEA/L.ROMANO/Contributor p125(bmr), deepblue4you p108(c), /d3sign/Moment p2, DGLimages p116(l), Design Pics/Ron Nickel p114(b), Devonyu p12(paper), Dorling Kindersley p90(l), dp3010 p115(golf), Dulin p50(5), farakos p12(router), Filo pp84, 85(background), Till Findl/EyeEm pp97(b), 133(mr), FGorgun p20(girl), FG Trade p18, fizkes p12(girl), fortise p77(3), fotog p104(r), franckreporter pp12,13 (background), David Freund pp46, 47(background), Shoji Fujita p20(rm), FUTURE LIGHT p96(c), gaffera p14(c), Gama5 p75(vase), Chris Griffiths p12(tapas), Eugene Gologursky/Stringer pp11(2), 51(t), Priscilla Gragg pp80(Luke), 115(boy), gremlin p75(br), Guerilla p47(tl), guvendemir pp96, 97(d), Handout p89(c), homydesign p75(hat), STAN HONDA/Staf p102, HRAUN p78(bl), Hulton Archive/Stringer p100(tr), ilyarexi p83(background), imageBROKER/Jurgen & Christine Sohns pp2(mr), 132, Image Source p24(Canes), Imgorthand p123, IsraelMckee p75(hat), Ivan p12(peppers), JTBC PLUS/Contributor p51(mr), Jose Luis Pelaez Inc p25(Hugo), Daniela Jovanovska-Hristovska p99(t), iStockphoto pp37(10), 65(a), 66(bl), 66(blc), 77(9), 108(d), 115(T-shirt), 116(brolly), iStockphoto/baibaz p108(h), Jupiterimages pp11(3), 97(g), Kitti Kahotong/EyeEm p75(tr), kajakiki p55(tm), Wattanaphob Kappago/EyeEm p77(7), Eva-Katalin p41(1), kate_sept2004 pp30, 80(Farouq), KeithBishop pp34, 35(background), Carina König/EyeEm p50(8), Jon Kopaloff/Stringer p84(a), JV Korotkova p68(tr), krung99 p68(mr), krungchingpixs pp58, 59, Suman Kumar/EyeEm p32(boy), Diane Labombarbe p27(rm), Lebedinski p52, LeoPatrizi p91(tr), Rob Lewine p18, LWA/Dann Tardif p24(evans), Sean Locke/EyeEm 47(bl), loops7p65(d), ludhi85 p47(tr), Anouk de Maar p15(ml), Regine Mahaux p83(4), Piotr Marcinski/EyeEm p25(Lena), Maskot p118(mel), maxkabakov p68(background), mayamo p37(2), Kevin Mazur/Contributor pp11, 20(tr), 130(tmr), Jamie McCarthy/Staff pp2, 59(tr), Natee Meepian p50(4), Meinzahn pp99(mr), 133(b), Luiz Henrique Mendes p37(b), Michael Mensch/EyeEm p15(tl), Jasmin Merdan p91(r), Mint Images p41(2), MirageC pp70, 71(background), Roberto Moiola/Sysaworld pp22, 23(background), monkeybusinessimages p35(bl), Julie Moquet/EyeEm p18, Morsa Images pp18, 25(Victor, Sandra, Ann, Paul), Multiart p108(b), NASA/Contributor p84(b), Zakharova_Natalia p37(5), Andrei Naumenka p77(2), Alexander/Nolting/EyeEm p96(f), NurPhoto/Contributor p109(l), OatmealStories p115(food), Micha Pawlitzki p32, Veronika Pfeiffer/EyeEm pp47(br), 131(t), phive2015 p37(3), Photodisc p47(tm), Plume Creative p25(Louise, Pierre), Martin Poole p27(b), popovaphoto p77(8), primeimages p17(tl), Fabio Principe p35(tc), Purestock/Punchstock p23(lm), ortonia p10(8), Marco Quintarelli/EyeEm p24(mac), Monty Rakusen p62(b), ribeirorocha p44(1), Tim Robberts p35(rm), rodrigobark p44(c), rolleiflextlr p77(6), Samuel de Roman/Contributor p89(lt), RossHelen p14(a), Royal/Geographical Society/Contributor 87(mr), Visit Roemvanitch/EyeEm p42(r), Nicolas Russell p31(2), SelectStock p31(1), selimaksan p24(Duffy), semenovp p37(d), Seva_blsv p59(2), Randy Shropshire/Stringer p28, Hugh Sitton p20(tl), skynesher p59(3), skytthyun/Imazins p77(4), smartboy10 pp106, 107(background), Artem Sokol 10(3), SolStock 101(r), OPA Images/Contributor p112, Henrik Sorensen p83(23), stocknroll p55(tl), STR/Stringer p63(mr), stu99 p97(e), Justin Sullivan/Staff p65(2), KOEN SUYK/Contributor p14(d), Tetra Images RF p118(Nina), TheCrimsonRibbon p56, ThinkDeep p123(cl), Yoshio Tomii p17(ml), Peter Unger p109(c), UniversalImagesGroup/Contributor 125(t), vectorforjoy p10(5), Klaus Vedfelt pp 3, 88(r), Mirko Vitali/EyeEm p80, Michael Webb/Stringer p88(l), Tom Werner pp41(4), 55(bm), Westend61 pp15(pea soup, bl), 27(t), 31(3), 35(tr), 35(lm), jun xu p(24(huang), TORU YAMANAKA/Staff p64, zhengzaishuru p23(tr); **gilaxia** p50(7); **Image Source**/FRAZER CUNNINGHAM p42(rc); **Macmillan Education Ltd** pp37(7), 65(f), 116(doll); **Madhave Lavakare** pp66(br, brc); **Mary Anning Rocks** – Registered Charity Number 1188919 pp90(lc), 133(mr); **Meghan Little/Cindy Goodman, North Shore News** pp39, 131(tr); **mikimad** p123(ml, c); Courtesy of **Thomas and Matthijs Molley** pp15(tr), 130(tr); Courtesy of **Morley** p89(r); **Iantha Naicker** pp11(7), 78(r); **PHOTODISC** p108(a); **PIXTAL** p10(bl); Courtesy of **Rongzhong Li, Petoi LLC** pp 2, 63(tr), 132(t); **Shutterstock.com** p108(g), Denis Belitsky p115(train), Cunaplus p10(1), Dreamworks/Universal/Kobal p87(tl), Elena11 p63(background), Granger p100(br), Fer Gregory p108(f), gststudio p10(2), J Chin/National Geographic/Kobal pp2(l), 87(c), 133(t), Jenson p62(background), judyjump p10(7), Larsvb p37(c), Stephen Lovekin p85(tl), oTTo-supertramp p68(bcl), Professional Bat p10(4), Santi S p123(tl), Silver Pictures/Kobal p13(Sherlock), Stas Malyarevsky p68(br), TurneroundDesigns p113(r), Twentieth Century Fox/Kobal p92, Wondervisuals p10(6), Xinhua News Agency p87(tr), Yayayoyo p89(1–5, a–f); **Spiral3Media**/Stuart Cox Photography pp48, 49, 131(mr); **Street Style Surgery LTD** p77(a, b, c, d, tcr); **Craig Teague**, Virtex Digital p113(cr); Courtesy of **UBTECH** pp11(5), 63(b); **Up the Resolution** p37(9).

Video footage and stills supplied by:
Digeo Productions pp13(r), 25(r), 61(br), 85(br); **DLA** pp3(rm), 37(r), 49(r), 73(r), 97(br); **MTJ** pp3(lm), 12(blm), 19(l, r), 24(blm), 31(tl), 36(blm), 43(l), 48(blm), 55(tl), 60(blm), 67(tl), 72(blm), 79(tl), 84(blm), 91(tl), 96(bml), 103(l); **Maia Films** pp3(tr), 12(bl), 22(l), 24(bl), 34(l), 36(bl), 46(l), 48(bl), 58(l), 60(bl), 70(l), 72(bl), 82(l), 84(bl), 94(l), 96(bl), 106(l).

Additional sources:
p10 – Statistics from BestCustomWriting.com website, 2012; Lyons, D. (2017). How Many People Speak English, And Where Is It Spoken?, Babbel.com; 5MinuteEnglish.com (2013). English Around the World; Smith, O. (2017). Mapped: Where to go if you can't be bothered to learn the language, *The Telegraph*.
p15 – Statistics from Adamson, P. (2013). Child Well-being in Rich Countries: A comparative overview, *Innocenti Report Card* no. 11, 3; 10 fun facts about the Netherlands, AwesomeAmsterdam.com, 2020; 25 interesting facts about the Netherlands, SwedishNomad.com, 2020.
p39 – Statistics from The Humane Society of the United States (2013). Meatless Monday: What a difference a day makes; nyp.org website, 2020; ThriveMeetings.com website, 2018; MeatFreeMondays.com website, 2016.
p40 – Statistics from Aviva (2018). 58% of parents believe lunches prepared at home are healthier than school dinners, but are they?; Isganaitis, E., Brown, F. and Ferris, H. (2017). People think juice is good for them. They're wrong, *Washington Post*.
p61 – Statistics from GuinnessWorldRecords.com website, 2020; Burke, K. (2016). 107 Texting Statistics That Answer All Your Questions, textrequest.com; Gokulan, D. (2016). World record holder plays 27 instruments at 23, khaleejtimes.com; Science Focus website, 2020; Davies, E. (2016). The greatest jumper on Earth is probably not a flea, BBC.com; Curiosity.com website, 2016.

Printed and bound in Brazil

2023
6